Cambridge Studies in Social Anthropology

NO. 3

KALAHARI VILLAGE POLITICS

Cambridge Studies in Social Anthropology

General Editors

M. FORTES, J. R. GOODY, E. R. LEACH, S. J. TAMBIAH

I

The Political Organization of Unyamwezi
by R. G. ABRAHAMS

2

*Buddhism and the Spirit Cults in
North-East Thailand*
by S. J. TAMBIAH

KALAHARI
VILLAGE POLITICS
An African Democracy

BY

ADAM KUPER

Lecturer in Social Anthropology
Makerere University College
Uganda

CAMBRIDGE
AT THE UNIVERSITY PRESS
1970

Published by the Syndics of the Cambridge University Press
Bentley House, 200 Euston Road, London N.W.1
American Branch: 32 East 57th Street, New York, N.Y. 10022

Library of Congress Catalogue Card Number: 70–112470

ISBN: 0 521 07863 6

FOR MY FATHER
THE LATE SIMON MEYER KUPER

Printed in Great Britain
at the University Press
Aberdeen

CONTENTS

TABLES

ILLUSTRATIONS

PLATES

MAPS

FIGURES

PREFACE

An apprenticeship in anthropology takes many years, and looking back I can see how fortunate I was in my teachers and guides. Professor John Blacking and Professor Max Marwick introduced me to social anthropology at the University of Witwatersrand and encouraged me to make it my career. At Cambridge I was privileged to work under Professor Meyer Fortes. I finally went to Botswana at the initiative of Professor Isaac Schapera, the doyen of Southern Bantu studies, and emboldened by the advice and instruction of Professor Ernst Westphal.

In my first attempt to analyse my field-data I benefited greatly from the constructive criticisms of Professor Schapera, Professor Fortes and Dr Ray Abrahams. A draft of the present book was read by Professor Fortes and Dr Peter Rigby, and with their help a number of important improvements were possible. My wife, Jessica, and my sister, Ruth Kuper, also made a number of useful suggestions.

I am indebted to Mrs Joyce Brown, who generously agreed to prepare the diagrams for this volume, and to Mrs T. Bailey, who did such a prompt and flawless job of the typing.

My initial field-study was facilitated by a grant from the Kalahari Research Committee, and I should particularly like to record my gratitude to their Chairman, Professor Philip Tobias. I was able to return to the Kalahari a second time with the help of grants from the H. Ling Roth fund, the Horniman fund, and the Esperanza trust. Throughout my apprenticeship my parents gave me unstinting support in every possible way. My wife, who shared only a brief part of the pleasures of field-work cheerfully endured the long period of analysis, writing, revision and proof-reading.

While I was in the Kalahari, I accumulated innumerable debts for hospitality and assistance which I despair of repaying. Mr George Silberbauer and Mr Simon Gillett, officers of the Government, were generous with invaluable advice, hospitality and friendship. Mr Peter Masire, Mr L. C. Sharp, Mr O. Saidoo and Mr J. Marumo eased the transition to Kalahari life and helped me endlessly throughout my stay in their country. The Ngologa themselves showed an almost super-human tolerance of my demands, and never allowed me to feel lonely or out of place. Mr Leswape Ramoswane, Mr Soblen Maayane and Mr Burupile Mojelaruri accepted me into the closest circle of friendship, and many, many other men and women will always remain in my heart.

Finally, I am grateful to the editors of *African Studies* and *Cahiers d'Études Africaines* for permitting me to use material which first appeared in their journals. Mr George Silberbauer has generously allowed me to include some material which I contributed to an article we published together.

ADAM KUPER

Makerere University College, Kampala
January 1969

NOTES ON PRESENTATION

No standard ŠiKgalagari orthography exists, and I have in general followed the usage of Van der Merwe and Schapera (1943 and 1945), which should be readily intelligible to students of Sotho languages.

The names of people and places are not disguised, except on the rare occasions when I am constrained to report something discreditable about a living person.

Finally, a minor point, although people in Botswana speak in terms of pounds, shillings and pence as well as rand and cents, I follow the official usage throughout. R1 = 11s. 9d. or $1.4.

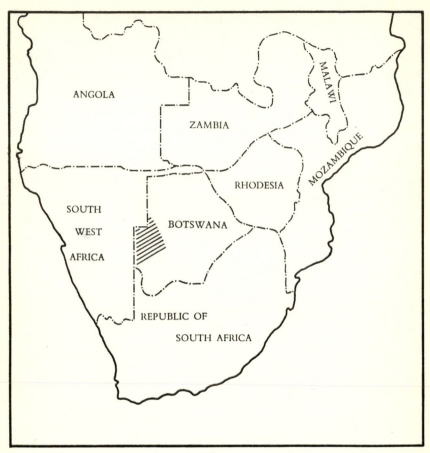

Map 1. Southern Africa. Shaded area indicates the region studied.

1

INTRODUCTION

I

Social anthropologists are often appealed to for a picture of 'traditional African society', despite the fact that their research activity has been concentrated within the last three or four decades. I am not sure where 'traditional society' is to be placed in time, but in most cases they were too late to observe it. In particular, few anthropologists have ever been in a position to study 'tribal' politics, except as modes of local government within colonial or settler states, or, more recently, independent states.[1] And yet, not least when dealing with politics, many anthropologists have accepted the role of antiquary and devoted their skills to the reconstruction of 'traditional tribal systems'; or, if they were historically-minded, to the evaluation of the ways in which 'western civilisation' has impinged on these 'traditional systems'. The analysis of modern political life in rural Africa, as a subject in its own right, has been neglected.

This is odd in view of the aggressively empirical ideology of modern social anthropology. Since Malinowski orthodox anthropologists have stressed the primary importance of direct observation. By implication the most suitable object of study is surely the contemporary situation. Some anthropologists have accepted this, but the general tendency has been to regard research into contemporary social reality as a special, even slightly disreputable, branch of social anthropology—the study of 'culture change'.

In 1938, for example, Fortes urged 'that the emphasis in current research should be placed upon the investigation of the dynamics of culture contact as this is actually observable in the field' (1938: 89).[2] He even gave some indication of how this precept might guide the study of local politics. Writing of what were then the undeveloped

[1] There are, even today, some African local political systems which are largely independent of the state, but they are rare. One example appears to be the Karimojong of Uganda—see Dyson-Hudson (1966), especially pp. 6–21 and 236–9.

[2] Malinowski was even blunter: 'Scientific observation can only be directed on what is; not on what might have been, or has been, even if this had vanished but yesterday. The scientific field-worker cannot study figments, and today an untouched native culture is only a figment.' (1938: xi.)

northern territories of the Gold Coast (now northern Ghana), he pointed out that:

With all that [the District Commissioner] stands for, he is a corporate part of native life in this area . . . The political and legal behaviour of the Tallensi, both commoner and chief, is as strongly conditioned by the ever-felt presence of the District Commissioner as by their own traditions. I made case-records in considerable detail, of all political and legal events which I was able to witness. In these one gets a glimpse of the concrete reaction of person upon person, the play of loyalties and hostilities, intrigues and counter-intrigues, intelligence and passion which constitute the reality of native institutions. And always, the District Commissioner, whether actually present or not, was one of the principal sanctions determining the outcome of events. (1938: 63.)

Yet after all, Fortes seems to have regarded the study of 'culture contact' (i.e. the observed reality) as of marginal importance compared with the reconstruction of the aboriginal culture. When he came to write in detail about Tallensi politics, he ignored the overarching framework of District Administration. While touching briefly on modern developments, he asserted that the 'foundations of the native social system remain intact', and was content to describe the 'indigenous political system' (1940: 240–1).

During the years which followed World War II, political anthropology was dominated by the study of segmentary lineage systems, and for a variety of reasons this central interest gave new strength to what might be called the never-never school of political anthropology. There were, however, some signs of rebellion. In retrospect, one of the most significant documents of the period was the paper on 'The Village Headman in British Central Africa' by Gluckman, Mitchell and Barnes, who were later to become leading figures in the 'Manchester School' of social anthropology. In this paper the authors developed the initial insight of Fortes, which I quoted earlier. They explored the modern context of village politics, and showed how the headman's role is moulded by the often-conflicting demands of his subjects and of the District Commissioner, between whom he occupies an 'intercalary' position.

The approach foreshadowed in this and other papers promised a new understanding of local politics in Africa, with due attention paid to the overarching context of the political systems. However, Gluckman and his colleagues preferred to follow other theoretical leads, and these lines of thought were left undeveloped. Gluckman and Barnes published path-finding studies in the field of African political history, and the members of the 'Manchester School' came to devote their attention to dramatic examples of recurrent political conflict—the feud, succession disputes, rebellions. This was not so much, perhaps, because these conflicts were believed to reveal the essence of political systems, as a reflection of their interest in the sociology of conflict itself. Later, particularly after the publication of Turner's *Schism and Continuity in an African Society*, in 1957, this broadened into a concern with 'total social processes', which were seen as processes of conflict and conflict resolution.

All this led away from the study of political systems. The emphasis was on the interplay of political events and other kinds of social events, a trend which led Easton, a political scientist, to complain in 1959 that 'Political institutions and practices tend to be viewed in anthropological research as independent variables, of interest primarily for their effect on other institutions and practices of the society of which they are part' (1959: 212–13).

In sum, those anthropologists who were concerned with modern social processes did not focus on the political system; while the anthropologists who did write about African political systems generally adopted a historical perspective, although this was often not made explicit. Both these approaches, of course, have their own validity, but the unfortunate consequence was that the daily stuff of modern politics went unrecorded—or at least unpublished.

Commenting on this situation, Southall has observed:

Many of us have been involved in the paradoxical irony that some of the most interesting and theoretically stimulating African political systems have been studied, as it were in amber, when they have almost ceased to exist. The real context of African political life has often been uninteresting to us, because it was colonial, as we were, therefore supposedly familiar. (1965: 135–6.)

The implication that anthropologists are interested only in the exotic may be embarrassing, but it obviously has some truth in it. In any case, it is a familiar enough accusation. There may also be something to say for the notion that 'the most interesting and theoretically stimulating African political systems . . . have almost ceased to exist'. Of greater significance, however, is the recognition of a connection between the shortcomings of political anthropology and the fact that anthropologists were working in a colonial framework. This raises the question, What will happen now that most of the formerly colonial territories are independent? Southall himself, and also Fallers and others, have suggested that now political anthropology will somehow be freed to study local politics in its contemporary context.[1] There is already considerable evidence of a resurgence of interest in African political anthropology, and one may also draw encouragement from the example of work by Bailey and others in India, which became independent earlier.

But although one must accept the importance of recent political developments in the revival of political anthropology, this is not the whole story. Anthropological theory, with its primarily functionalist orientation, was ill-adapted to the analysis of the interaction of a political system and its environment, and this was precisely the area which political anthropology had to explore if it was to deal with local politics in a realistic fashion. In the last few years, anthropologists have found a new stimulus in the work of American political science, which has been experiencing something of a renaissance. At a conference of social anthropologists held in 1963, all the papers on political anthropology referred to works in political science, a novel phenomenon on which Gluckman and Eggan commented rather sourly in their introductory review. The authority cited most frequently was Easton, whose theories are rapidly being absorbed into social anthropology.[2]

The research on which the present book is based was carried out during this period of political revolution and theoretical reorientation. I began my field-work among the Kgalagari in 1963, and completed it in 1967, with an interval during which I wrote my doctoral dissertation. This book emerged slowly from the confrontation of my observations of Kgalagari politics and society with the new developments in anthropological theory and in African politics.

II

It was Professor Schapera who suggested that I might make a study of the Kgalagari-speaking peoples of Botswana (then the Bechuanaland Protectorate, one of the three British High Commission Territories in southern Africa). The material available on the Kgalagari was sparse, much of it scattered as asides in reports of missionaries, administrators

[1] Southall, 1965: 135–6; Fallers, 'Political Sociology and the Anthropological Study of African Politics' (1963).
[2] The papers on political anthropology are collected in *Political Systems and the Distribution of Power* (1965).

and travellers.[1] This was scarcely surprising. The small African communities in western Botswana have always been administered from a confortable distance. There are no missions working among them. And the Kgalagari lack the romantic appeal of the Bushmen, who have attracted several anthropologists to the Kalahari.

The reports of the late nineteenth and early twentieth centuries described the Kgalagari as poor, degenerate Tswana, representatives of the first wave of Sotho migration to southern Africa. It was generally assumed that the later waves of Tswana migrants had pushed them into the Kalahari, relieved them of their livestock, and reduced them to servitude. The poverty and generally miserable condition of the Kgalagari was often stressed, but some early accounts suggest that while temporarily forced back on a hunting and gathering way of life, the Kgalagari retained the ambition to be pastoralists. Many Kgalagari, particularly in the east of Botswana, remained serfs until after World War I. Their condition was evidently better than that of Bushman serfs, but, as one writer remarked, although 'the lot of these vassals is just bearable in time of peace, it is beyond conception wretched in time of war'. (Mackenzie, 1871: 132.)

In 1938 Schapera published his discovery that the language of the people, ŠiKgalagari, was not a Tswana dialect, as had previously been assumed, but an independent member of the Sotho language family. This gave a jolt to received ideas, and stimulated new research. In 1944 Dr D. F. van der Merwe made a brief field-trip to the central Kalahari and carried out an analysis of ŠiKgalagari which confirmed Schapera's findings. Professor Westphal, who has done further linguistic work in the Kalahari in recent years, agrees that the language is distinct from SeTswana, and adds that the linguistic evidence associates the Kgalagari with the first Sotho migrations to southern Africa.[2]

At the same time the first reliable evidence on Kgalagari culture and traditions was provided by the linguistic texts which Schapera and van

---

[1] Some of the early sources on the Kgalagari are the diaries and letters of Livingstone, which have recently been edited by Schapera and published by Chatto and Windus, and the publications of travellers like Chapman and Farini. More systematic treatment, based mainly on these and similar secondary sources, can be found in G. W. Stow, *The Native Races of South Africa*, published in 1905. Breutz, 'Ancient People in the Kalahari Desert' (1958), includes a useful review of the literature and a full bibliography.

[2] I. Schapera, 'Ethnographic Texts in the Boloongwe Dialect of Sekgalagadi' (1938); D. F. van der Merwe and I. Schapera, *A Comparative Study of Kgalagadi, Kwena and other Sotho Dialects* (1943); and E. Westphal, 'The Linguistic Prehistory of Southern Africa' (1963).

2

der Merwe collected and published.[1] Schapera drew two main conclusions from this material. First, he remarked that 'although the
Kgalagadi dialects (despite local variations) form a single group, the
people speaking those dialects do not seem to have a single origin'.
Secondly, while the Kgalagari could not be regarded any longer merely
as poor, degenerate Tswana, the evidence suggested that Kgalagari
culture was very similar to Tswana culture. He would not commit
himself, however, as to whether these resemblances stemmed from
borrowing, resulting from long and close contact, or whether the
Tswana and Kgalagari represented offshoots of 'the same basic culture'.[2]

III

In short, the literature presented a gloomy picture of Kgalagari life,
and suggested only two problems for further research: the relationship
between Kgalagari and Tswana culture; and the antecedents of the
various Kgalagari groups.[3] My own interests, however, ran in the
direction of contemporary social life and politics rather than culture
history. Accordingly my first priority was to find a suitable social field.

In mid-1963 I made a brief exploratory tour of the Kalahari. I found
that the Kgalagari-speaking peoples in the western Crown Lands (now
State Lands) live in scattered village communities, each of which
enjoys a high degree of political autonomy. This was in contrast to the
situation of the Kgalagari in the east of the country, who are under
Tswana rule. The largest Kgalagari group in the State Lands are the
Ngologa. They conceive of themselves as one people, and are concentrated in an arc of settlements in Northern Kgalagadi and Ghanzi
Districts. Working on the usual assumption that one's chosen social
field should have geographical and cultural unity, I decided to make a
study of the Ngologa in this area.

The origins of the Ngologa remain something of a puzzle. They
moved into the Kalahari in the course of the nineteenth century.[4]

[1] Especially I. Schapera and D. F. v. d. Merwe, *Notes on the Tribal Groupings, History,
and Customs of the Bakgalagadi* (1945).   [2] Schapera and v. d. Merwe 1938: 20–23.

[3] On this latter point, Dr P.-L. Breutz visited the Kgalagari 'to see to what extent the
non-Bantu population may have originated from ancient races [*sic*] and whether they
could be remnants of the stone kraal builders in South Africa' (1958: 55). Handicapped
as he was by the brevity of his stay and the eccentricity of his preoccupations, Breutz's
conclusions are mainly of curiosity value.

[4] 'Kalahari' is an anglicisation of Kgalagari. It seems probable that the desert is named
after the people, rather than vice versa, since there are people called Kgalagari elsewhere, including one group in Lesotho. It is common for Sotho-speaking peoples to
name a country after its inhabitants—e.g. the Kweneng is the country of the Kwena.

Many of them trace their ancestors to Thaba Nchu, in the Orange Free State, and to the northern Cape, but more immediately they were settled in what is now eastern Botswana. They probably emerged in their contemporary form during the anarchic decades of the early nineteenth century, when groups of Kgalagari serfs deserted their Tswana masters and moved west into the Kalahari, establishing new, politically independent communities. This was the period—between about 1810 and 1840—when

> there prevailed among the Tswana a period of chaos, due initially in some tribes to civil wars, but mainly to the successive onslaughts of invaders from the east, notably the MmaNtatisi (1822–3), Sebetwane's Kololo (1823–8), and Moselekatse's Tebele (1825–37). During this time some of the Tswana tribes were forced to flee from their homes, to which they did not return until the danger was past; others, less fortunate, were irretrievably broken up into scattered groups that managed to survive only by attaching themselves permanently to other tribes. (Schapera, 1953: 15.)

It is uncertain whether the Ngologa were already a united group with some sense of identity at the time of their westward flight. Some oral traditions suggest that various groups were united during this period by a Rolong (Tswana) aristocrat. In any case, they incorporated some groups who were already in the Kalahari.

Groups of Ngologa had regularly grazed their herds and hunted in the central Kalahari during the rainy seasons, and when they fled they knew they were going to a place where they would find a few natural springs and large herds of game. Most of them settled in the Matšeng area, within a radius of about 50 miles of the modern Hukuntsi. From the first they were organised in several separate and independent political communities. The people they found in occupation, small bands of Bushmen and members of other ethnic groups, whose identity remains shadowy,[1] were integrated into the new communities or pushed aside. Many of the Bushmen became serfs.

The Ngologa at Matšeng soon entered into trading relations with Tswana groups in the Cape Colony, including those around the London Missionary Society station at Kuruman, and also with peoples in eastern Botswana. They carried skins of wild animals south and east and returned with some livestock and other goods. This gradual accumulation of wealth through trading, together with occasional raids, may have enabled them slowly to re-establish themselves as

[1] Breutz speculates about their origin and identity (1958), but does not carry much conviction.

pastoralists, although the main spurt of economic rehabilitation appears to have occurred only in the last sixty years or so. There were Ngologa living a nomadic life with small herds of goats, dependent on hunting and gathering, until the first decades of the twentieth century, and in some cases even more recently.

Although the Ngologa were often badly treated by their Tswana trading partners, they borrowed many new ideas from them. Through Tswana contacts some Ngologa were brought into touch with the London Missionary Society station at Kuruman. According to one version, an individual Ngologa porter became interested in Christianity, was trained at Kuruman, and returned to the Kalahari to convert his fellows, so initiating an enduring relationship between the Ngologa and the London Missionary Society. It was evidently also from their Tswana trading contacts that the Ngologa learnt the art of sinking bucket-wells. These were superior to the primitive sip-wells on which they had previously relied, and they made possible Ngologa colonisation of pans west of Matšeng.

The late nineteenth and early twentieth century was a period of turmoil in southern Africa, marked by large-scale movements of population. It was not long before the area recently settled by the Ngologa was invaded by new groups, Tswana (Rolong and Tlharo) from the south and east, and Herero and Hottentots from the new German colony in the west. There were several clashes between these groups. The names of two pans near Hukuntsi, Bohelo Bathyo and Bohelo Batšwana (The Last of People and The Last of Children) recall massacres of Ngologa at the hands of the Hottentots. The Rolong and Tlharo asserted a right to rule the Ngologa, even to make them serfs, which led to disputes lasting for many years. (In some parts of the Kalahari this nuisance was at last solved only by Government intervention in the 1930s and 1940s.)

Soon the pressure of population began to squeeze the modest natural resources of Matšeng. Groups of Ngologa moved away, occupying pans in the west and north, in what is now Ghanzi District and in Ngamiland. This second wave of migration coincided with colonial involvement in south-western Africa. The Ngologa migrants, who covered ground rapidly, ran up against European colonies in German West Africa and at Ghanzi. Their movement was checked and diverted. Some Ngologa were turned out of Ghanzi by a British official at the end of the nineteenth century. A few years later, groups of Ngologa who had entered German West Africa returned to the new British protectorate in Bechuanaland.

The British protectorate over Bechuanaland was proclaimed in 1885, and in 1898 the first European colony in the Kalahari was officially set up at Ghanzi. Although neither settlement nor administration was carried on with great vigour, the British presence was soon firmly established, and the restless population movements of the nineteenth century gradually came to an end. By the 1920s, the African communities in the Kalahari were for the most part settled in the areas they occupy today. The Ghanzi Europeans periodically made representations to the Government to the effect that the whole of Ghanzi District had been promised to them as an area of white settlement, and that African farmers (though not Bushman servants) should be kept out. Notwithstanding these pressures, the African settlements were allowed to remain and even to expand, at any rate once the small groups of African pioneers had been cleared out of the Ghanzi farming area itself.

Ghanzi and Kgalagadi Districts have today a combined population of about 32,700 in an area of 82,800 square miles. (The two Districts are of roughly equal size, and each has about the same population.) Together they account for about 6 per cent of Botswana's population and 38 per cent of its total area. There are roughly 9,000 Bushmen in these Districts, and there are also about 2,000 European and Coloured ranchers. Of perhaps 20,000 Bantu-speaking peoples, about 10,000 live in the belt of settlements in Ghanzi and northern Kgalagadi District with which I am concerned here.

These Bantu groups are concentrated in an arc of ten villages (with some hamlets) which stretches from Kang in the north-east of Kgalagadi District westwards into Ghanzi District and then north to Kalkfontein, the northernmost Bantu village in Ghanzi District. A track for lorries and four-wheel drive vehicles runs about 300 miles along this arc from Kang to Kalkfontein, passing through Matšeng, Nojane and Kuli. It joins up with tracks to the more developed eastern centres of Botswana and to the District capitals, Ghanzi and Tsabong.

Roughly 6,000 of these 10,000 Bantu villagers are Ngologa. Other Kgalagari groups which are represented here are the Kgwateng, who are often identified as Ngologa, and the Šaga. In addition, there are Tswana of the Rolong and Tlharo groups, Herero, and small communities of settled non-Bantu Bushmen and Hottentots.

Seven of the ten villages are ruled by Kgalagari-speaking peoples, six by Ngologa and one by Šaga. Two of the other villages are ruled by Tswana headmen but have Ngologa majorities. The remaining

Table 1. *The composition of Bantu villages in Ghanzi District and northern Kgalagadi District* (1967)[1]

Name of village	Population*	Headman's name and ethnic group	Ethnic composition (groups are named in order of size)
		GHANZI DISTRICT	
1. Kalkfontein	1,470	Tšekwe (Ngologa)	Kgalagari (Ngologa) Herero
2. Karakobis	831	Matlamme (Tlharo)	Kgalagari (Ngologa) Tswana (Rolong and Tlharo) Herero
3. Makunda	1,035	Kavangyere (Herero)	Herero Bushmen
4. Kuli	448	Ramošwane (Ngologa)	Kgalagari (Ngologa) Bushmen
5. Nojane	1,480	Keakopa (Tlharo)	Kgalagari (Ngologa) Tswana (Rolong and Tlharo) Hottentots Bushmen
		NORTHERN KGALAGADI DISTRICT	
6. Tshane	630	Mosalaengwe (Ngologa)	Kgalagari (mainly Ngologa) Hottentots Bushmen
7. Hukuntsi	2,030	Moapare (Ngologa) [sub-chief]	Kgalagari (Ngologa) Tswana (Rolong and Tlharo)
8. (a) Lehututu	1,350	Leswape II (Ngologa)	Kgalagari (Ngologa and Šaga) Bushmen
(b) Hamlets of Lehututu	389	(Monong, Ncaa and Ohe)	Kgalagari (Ngologa) Bushmen
9. Lokgwabe	964	Oloatse (Kgwateng)	Kgalagari (Kgwateng and other Ngologa) Hottentots
10. Kang	647	(*Vacant*—Šaga)	Kgalagari (Šaga)
Total population	11,274		

* Source: *Report on the Census of the Bechuanaland Protectorate* (1964).

Note on classification: As I mentioned earlier, the Kgwateng are usually classified with the Ngologa in the Kalahari, while the Šaga are distinguished from them. So far as the Bushmen are concerned, I have included only the Bushmen settled in or near the villages, and use this vague and general category to include the Lala, whose ethnic status is uncertain, and also the Naron, who, linguistically, are perhaps better classified as Hottentots.

[1] For the distribution of Kgalagari groups in eastern and northern Botswana, see Schapera, *The Ethnic Composition of Tswana Tribes* (1952). Some information on the distribution of the Kgalagari in the Republic of South Africa is contained in Breutz, 1958.

village is ruled and occupied by Herero. In short, the Ngologa constitute a majority in eight of the ten villages, and rule six of them.

The present distribution of Bantu communities in Ghanzi District
and northern Kgalagadi District is set out in Table 1, and in Map 2.

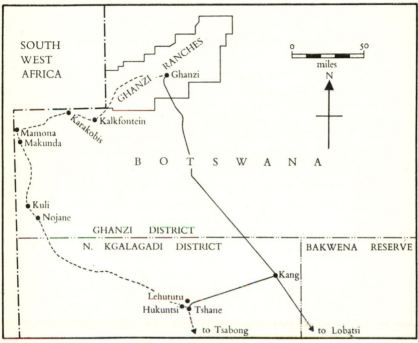

Map 2. Bantu villages in the Kalahari Districts of Botswana.

IV

The country in which the Ngologa live is not inhospitable, and generations of visitors have suggested that the Kalahari's desolate reputation
is not fully deserved. In a letter written in 1850, David Livingstone
made this point, although he did suggest that life was not easy there:

The Desert does not deserve the name, except from its great want of water,
for it is usually covered with abundance of grass, bushes, and trees. Nor is it
destitute of inhabitants. Both men and animals exist in considerable numbers.
Man, however, has a hard struggle to keep soul & body together. The
Bakalahari children are usually distinguished by the large protruding
abdomen and thin ill-formed legs & arms. The listless eye shews that youth
has few joys for them. Although much oppressed by the Bechuanas [i.e.,
Tswana] who visit them annually in order to collect skins, they are often at
variance among themselves. (1961: 160.)

More recently, a commission of experts remarked that 'perhaps the most striking impression was that this was no Sahara but an endless panorama of grass and bush growing in a mantle of sand and repeated over the whole immense area of some 50 million acres'. They selected for special mention the western section of the country occupied by the Ngologa—

A particularly good piece of country seemed to lie between latitude 23° and 24°. From about twenty-five miles north-west of Tsane, right up to Makunda, and especially around Ukwi pan, we were impressed by the balance of shady tree, edible shrub and variety of grasses. The belt seemed to continue south-westwards to the frontier of South-West Africa.[1]

The areas which they excluded from this general enthusiasm are those which have been densely settled and over-grazed, for the ecological balance in the Kalahari is delicate, and true desert may easily take over.

In short, the area is suitable for cattle and rich in game. Grazing is particularly good, and some agricultural activity is possible, although the soil is poor. The drawback is the scarcity of water. Except for brief periods after rainstorms, there is no surface water, and the rainfall is low and unreliable.[2]

With the exception of the hunting and gathering Bushmen, the people of the Kalahari base their economy on their herds of cattle and goats. They also grow a few crops, with intermittent success, and hunt and trap game. To raise extra cash they sell hides and skins, or go abroad as migrant labourers. But their most valued and valuable goods are their cattle. As a result of the spiralling demand for beef and cattle by-products in the industrialised areas of southern Africa, the people of the Kalahari are no longer the destitute wretches of earlier descriptions.

To meet the needs of their herds, cattle-owners must settle near reliable, perennial and generous sources of water. However, suitable sites are rare, which explains why settlements in the Kalahari are so few in number and so scattered. In general, the only solution is to settle around the pans, the famous depressions of the Kalahari, which are

---

[1] *Report of a Mission to the Bechuanaland Protectorate to investigate the possibilities of economic development in the West Kalahari* (H.M.S.O., 1954). Quotations are from pp. 3–4.

[2] Annual rainfall in inches for the years 1961 to 1965 was as follows:

	1965	1964	1963	1962	1961	Norm
Tshane	6·07	4·28	17·08	6·11	17·65	10·98
Ghanzi	11·77	6·75	30·86	9·84	15·00	17·85

(Source: *Bechuanaland: Report for the Year 1965*.)

thought to mark fossil water-courses. Wells sunk in these pans may strike water at a depth of only twenty to fifty feet, and water may be trapped on the surface for days on end during the rains. These ecological imperatives go a long way towards explaining the outstanding features of Kalahari village politics, their independence of each other and the high level of participation in public affairs.[1]

V

My initial decision to study the Kgalagari was largely due to accident, but once it was made the choice of the Ngologa for special considera-tion was straightforward. Now, on the completion of my tour of inspection, I decided that the Ngologa *village community* should be the primary focus of my study.

This choice was to some extent forced upon me by the situation of the Kalahari villages. As I have indicated, the villages are clearly defined, isolated units, islands of dense human settlement in the desert. Everyone has a sense of belonging to a particular village, and of the village as a community. People interact with fellow-villagers in a variety of situations every day, while it is an effort to visit kinsmen and friends in other villages. Each village is also, in a sense, an economic corporation, and, most important for my purposes, it constitutes a political unit under its own headman. In the mid-1950s, the Govern-ment created the Hukuntsi headman a 'sub-chief' (moving him up an administrative grade), and gave him authority over the headmen of Lehututu, Tshane, Lokgwabe and Kang. Even these villages, however, retain a good deal of independence in the management of their com-munal affairs. The villages in Ghanzi District remain distinct political corporations, no authority intervening between the headmen and the District Administration.

But my choice also fitted in with a current trend in social anthro-pology. There has been a move away from the study of 'cultures' or 'tribes'. Many anthropologists now prefer to lay their emphasis on the study of process within a social field, which is usually defined in practice as a community of manageable size. The goal is to uncover the social dynamics of a community rather than to describe the outlines of a 'culture', or to analyse the 'total social structure of a society' (by which is often meant a 'tribe'). In some respects this involves only a

---

[1] Cf. Schapera, *Government and Politics in Tribal Societies* (1956), p. 210. For further information on the pans and other features of the ecology, see Debenham, *Kalahari Sand* (1953).

slight shift in orientation, but it does imply 'a different kind of field-work [from that of the post-Malinowski generation], viz. more intensive research within a smaller unit' (Van Velsen, 1967: 145).

Advocates of this new approach (variously termed the extended-case method and situational analysis) have had to justify the relevance of such microscopic studies. Gluckman has suggested that, with the help of statistical techniques, one can establish the ways in which one's social field is typical of the 'tribe', and so attempt to generalise outwards from, say, the village to the society as a whole.[1] Van Velsen prefers to play down the importance of making general statements about the 'tribe' in the classical anthropological fashion. He argues that situational analysis might rather 'yield the kind of material that will enable us to lay a better foundation for large-scale cross-cultural comparison' (1967: 146). I was not sure whether I was looking for a microcosm of humanity or merely of 'the Ngologa', but I was confident of the usefulness of a study in depth of one or perhaps two villages. At the least I could expect to bring back an understanding of the political process at the community level which would be a useful supplement to the first-class studies of large-scale southern Bantu political systems already available.

My first period of field-work was in 1963–4. During this time I spent about twelve months in the Kalahari villages, including eight to nine months in one village, Kuli. In addition I spent some time at Government stations, visiting other parts of Botswana and so forth.

Kuli, which was my base, is located in the extreme south of Ghanzi District, a dozen miles east of the South West African border and a few miles north of the Tropic of Capricorn. It is far from any urban centre or European settlement, lying about sixty miles south of the road which travels from Ghanzi, the District capital, to Gobabis in South West Africa, the nearest town and rail-head. Lacking even a store, Kuli had the great attraction for me of romantic isolation. It also had technical advantages—it was of manageable size, situated in the middle of the arc of Kalahari Bantu settlements, and predominantly Ngologa in composition. The main village settlement is occupied entirely by Ngologa, who number about 350. The remainder of the population (which totals about 450) are Bushmen, who live in two settlements on the outskirts of the village.

Before leaving England I had taken an introductory course in SeTswana with Professor Westphal, then of the School of Oriental and

---

[1] M. Gluckman, 'Ethnographic Data in British Social Anthropology' (1961).

African Studies. Within about six months I was fairly fluent in conversation. Moreover, I went to Kuli after spending seven weeks with a trader in Kalkfontein, during which time I learnt something about the Ngologa way of life and made friends with a number of people in the District. By the time I came to Kuli, I was therefore in a position to begin productive field-work.

The headman of Kuli lent me a hut within his family-group site. This was near the centre of the village, and I was well placed to observe the day-to-day comings and goings of the people. I was within a few yards of the headman's compound, the *kgota* (council-place), the school, the church and the village borehole. The villagers soon accepted my presence and they showed me great friendliness throughout my stay. I stress these matters because if the situation had been less satisfactory I might have been tempted, even at this late stage, to retire from 'situational analysis' to a more detached and wide-ranging cultural survey. The direction of social anthropological research is often determined as much by accident and serendipity as by theoretical considerations.

VI

I had chosen to do a situational analysis of village social life, under the influence of the thinking of the 'Manchester School', and those circumstances moulded the themes of my research. I retained my interest in village politics, but willy-nilly I was faced with the characteristic problems of sorting out multiplex relationships, and working out the interaction of political events and events in other domains of social life.

The village is made up of co-residential units based on kinship. These groups are the primary social units, and they operate at times as political factions. A man's allegiance is, however, directed also to the village community. All the Ngologa men are citizens and participate in the public affairs of the village. The Ngologa themselves have two basic modes of conceptualising social relationships. One is in terms of domestic relationships, kinship and affinity; the other in terms of the political community and citizenship. These are roughly compatible with the sociological opposition between the politico-jural and domestic domains of social relationship. Each domain is characterised by a specific set of values and patterns of behaviour. At the same time, there is a dialectical interaction between events in the two domains, and also between kinship status and political status, neither of which is strictly ascribed or achieved, but rather reflects individual manipulation of conventionally limited possibilities.

In 1966, in the course of an extended break from the field, I attempted a preliminary analysis of my material in these terms. The problem as it appeared at that stage was to identify the domestic–kinship and the politico–jural domains of social action within the village, and to analyse the impact of events in the kinship domain on politics, and vice versa.[1] It soon became apparent that this was, at best, only a first step towards the understanding of village politics. I was vulnerable to Easton's criticism that anthropologists tend to treat politics as an independent variable rather than as a primary isolate. As a consequence of this, I was not paying sufficient attention to the essentials of village politics— the formulation and processing of political demands. Moreover, I had still to come to terms with the external forces which impinged on Kalahari village politics. An ideal analysis would isolate the village political system, without violently detaching it from its domestic and external environment.

These considerations seem obvious enough, but I became aware of them only then, partly because I felt I was not doing justice to the complexity of the situation I had observed, but also in response to new theoretical and political developments. I have already mentioned the new theoretical vitality of political anthropology in the mid-sixties, stimulated by American political science. More sophisticated analytical frameworks were now available, and a new realism was abroad. On the political front, Britain's southern African territories were being hurried towards independence. In this changed setting the overarching political and administrative structure seemed to acquire greater visibility. An essay on Kalahari village politics which ignored this dimension was now clearly unreal and irrelevant to contemporary Africa. And so I returned to the Kalahari, this time with rather clearer objectives.

VII

I spent a further five months in the field between October 1966 and April 1967. During this period Botswana became an independent state, the system of local government was reformed, and new factors entered into village politics. These were the elements of a crucial modern African experience which had been enacted in other countries in the continent over the past few years.

[1] The argument is summed up in my paper, 'The Kinship Factor in Ngologa Politics' (1969).

Most of my field-work on this second visit, as on the first, was done in Kuli. This concentration on the events in a single village permits of a certain continuity and time-depth in many of the cases I cite. As a politico-administrative unit, and a Ngologa village, however, Kuli has much in common with other Kalahari villages. I have not hesitated to introduce material collected in other villages where it seems useful. On the other hand, broader ethnographic comparisons with other southern Bantu communities, or with communities further abroad, are foreign to my purpose here, which is primarily descriptive and analytic.

The main political institutions in the Kgalagari village are the headmanship and the village council, the assembly of citizens. The key decision-making body is the *lekgota*, the headman-in-council, and the *lekgota* itself is dominated by an inner circle of influential citizens, who constitute the 'village authority'. The selection of political office-holders and the structure of alliances within the *lekgota* are in large part a function of active kinship relationships within the village. The headmanship and the *lekgota* are not simply village institutions, how-ever; they are also part of the national system of local government. The environment of the system is thus provided by the overarching structure of local government and by the social organisation of the villagers.

Political demands and support, which constitute the 'inputs' of the political system, are mediated by the citizen body or by groups within it, and by the District authorities, or, more recently, the Democratic Party. These groups are the keepers of the political threshold, and constitute the immediate intra-societal and extra-societal environment of the village political system. Decisions, policies, administrative actions, the 'outputs' of the system, are absorbed by the same groups, and may in turn generate new demands or produce changes in the structure of support.[1]

The following chapter deals with the village social setting. In Chapter 3 I discuss the District Administration and District politics, and indicate the lines of communication between the villagers and these external authorities. Chapter 4 sets out the political structure of the village community—political institutions, roles and groups. Chapter 5 is concerned with the content of village politics. The remaining chapters are devoted to the political process.

At various points I shall take up problems of anthropological theory,

[1] Easton's influence may be apparent in this formulation.

but only as they impinge on my analysis. I am not concerned primarily
to test and modify particular hypotheses. My aim is to describe and
analyse contemporary local politics in this remote, but not atypical,
part of Africa.

It may seem rather pointless to devote so much energy to the study
of mini-politics, and indeed the affairs of the Kalahari villages are
parochial by any standards. But as Leys, a political scientist, pointed
out in 1967, students of African politics have learnt 'remarkably little
about politics outside the capitals, where 95 per cent of the populations
live'. This lack of information is crucial in countries where effective
centralisation is still in the future. Leys himself, in an essay on politics in
Acholi District, Uganda, attempted 'to find out something about
politics in a newly independent African state from the point of view of
the voter in the countryside, rather than that of the political élite in the
towns'. Unfortunately he chose to concentrate on District affairs, and
as he admits the result 'is not the point of view of the rural voter. It is a
fragmentary glimpse of some of the political concerns of the district
élite.' (Preface to Leys, 1967.) The present work represents a social
anthropologist's attempt to explore the same problem at a lower level
of political activity. I believe that in many ways Kuli and the other
Kalahari villages represent the elementary form of local government
and politics in Africa. If I am correct, my analysis may serve as a
sketch towards a paradigm of such systems.

2

THE VILLAGE

I

The Kalahari villages are focused on pans. Some are built in a circle of which the pan is the hub, like Kalkfontein or Nojane, which schoolboys call 'Round City',while others are built in an irregular arc around part of the pan, like Kuli. Although a degree of compactness is forced on the villages by the need to settle near the wells which are sunk in the pan, the villages of all tribal groups in the Kalahari are more diffuse than villages in eastern Botswana. This is in part a function of lower population pressure, but it also reflects the limited power of the head-man. Village headmen sometimes try to persuade their subjects to move their homes close together, but usually without effect. Compounds within a family group may be sixty to a hundred yards apart, and family-groups are often out of sight of their nearest neighbours, several hundred yards away across uncleared bush. The layout of the village represents a compromise between the centripetal attraction of the pan and centrifugal social forces.

Small permanent settlements at pans near a village may fall within the headman's jurisdiction, while enjoying greater independence than any section of the main village. These hamlets should be distinguished from the outposts, cattle-posts and gardens, which some villagers maintain for a part of each year. The outposts are generally within easy distance of the village, although wealthy men, particularly in over-populated areas like Matseng, may keep up distant cattle-posts. A man rarely stays at his outpost for long periods, and most keep members of their family in the village, visiting them regularly and attending sessions of the village council (*lekgota*).

There are also permanent or seasonal Bushman camps on the out-skirts of some villages. These Bushmen lead their own lives for the most part, hunting, gathering veldkos, and in some cases even looking after their own small gardens and some livestock. Bushmen living in the vicinity of the villages are, however, usually also serfs of Bantu masters, and spend some of their time herding for the citizens of the villages or doing seasonal work for them.

The village itself is divided into several spatially distinct groups of compounds, interspersed with gardens, chicken-runs, and small kraals for milch-cows and calves, and for goats. The largest divisions, which I call sectors, are occupied by a Ngologa sub-clan or a segment of a foreign tribe. Each sector is named for the sub-clan occupying it—e.g. *Gapebana*, the place of the Pebana clan. Not all sub-clans are solidary groups concentrated in one sector of the village, but where this is the case the sub-clan has administrative and political functions.

Within the sectors (and outside them) there are smaller units which I call family-groups. They are made up of several compounds, often arranged in an arc or rough oval about a central focus such as a shady tree. The land within the family-group site is usually grassless and arid, indicating the high concentration of people and animals. The family-group typically comprises a group of kin clustered about an agnatic core. The senior agnate in the core group is usually the group head, and the group takes its name from him—e.g. *kgota wa i go Haudwelwe*, Haudwelwe's family-group (or family-group site).

A compound is made up of one or more huts encircled by a fence, and it is usually occupied by the members of a nuclear family, or a matrifocal unit. Widows and the various wives of polygamists usually have their own households, each with its own small estate of domestic equipment, perhaps a garden, poultry and domestic animals. Young unmarried men and women participate in the economic activities of the parental compound, although they may have their own huts outside the fence.

These local units can be recognised fairly easily, and the Ngologa distinguish each of them in certain contexts. However, there are no unambiguous terms for them. *Moze* may mean a town (like Ghanzi), a village, a hamlet, a sector, or even a family-group. *Legaya* (which carries some of the connotations of the English word 'home') may similarly be applied to any of these settlements, and also to a compound or a hut. The term *kgota* has an even wider range of meaning. It is applied not only to sectors and family-groups, but also to any patrilineal grouping.[1]

Most of the social groupings within the village are organised on kinship principles and are anchored in these local units. An understanding of their structure and of the ideology associated with them is

[1] Several writers have commented on the ambiguity of Sotho terms for local groupings. See Sheddick, 1948: 31, and Schapera, 1935: 204–5.

1. A homestead.

2. A well on Kuli pan.

3. The school at Kuli.

4. *Ipelegeng:* building a store-house at the school.

important if one is to fathom village politics, and I shall discuss them at some length in this chapter. I begin with the Ngologa 'models' of these groupings, which provides the idiom and ideology of much of their social life. Then I present a sociological view of their structure which, while equally an abstraction, has a certain explanatory value. Finally I describe the composition and organisation of the social groupings in Kuli village over a period of time.

II

When an anthropologist describes the folk theories of a society there is always a danger of intrusive rationalisation, for these theories may be imperfectly integrated. Different, even contradictory, elements may be stressed at different times. In an attempt to minimise this danger I will concentrate on the elucidation of three key concepts, *širethyo*, *kgota* and *lošitša*.

Širethyo can mean 'totem', but it also connotes the Ngologa as a whole (or, occasionally, another people), or any clan. The Ngologa people and the various clans are conceived of as patrilineages. All Ngologa are said to be descended from a group of brothers, the senior of whom was Mongologa, the hero-founder of Ngologa society. Each brother was the founder of a clan. Apart from the Ngologa clan,[1] most clans are named for totems, and the 'founder' is spoken of as the person-of-the-totem—e.g. *Mothyaga*, the man-of-the-finch. (Some informants say that the clan ancestors were Mongologa's sons, not his brothers. However, the role of father and senior brother is similar in Ngologa society.)

Informants provide varying lists of the Ngologa clans, at least partly depending on where they come from, for some clans are not known or are unimportant in some parts of the country. Nevertheless everyone agrees on the ranking of clans relative to each other. The clan's rank is related to the position of its ancestor in the founding fraternity. Some small clans are regarded as linked to major clans, from which they are said to have separated because of quarrels with agnates.

While the members of a clan think of themselves as sharing a common heritage, the clans are not action groups. Clan members are dispersed between several villages and never join as a group for any purpose. Each clan has a totem, which usually gives it its name, but aside from

---

[1] The Ngologa clan, while the senior, is like other clans, and its members do not have a special status. No village is controlled by members of this clan, although they did once rule Lehututu.

totemic avoidances, which are not insisted upon, they do not have ritual unity.[1]

The clan model has several functions. It charts broad social categories and so facilitates the categorisation of people. Any Ngologa may be placed with reference to this pan-Ngologa scheme. A man from a senior clan is 'elder brother' and a man from a junior 'younger brother'. Members of one's own clan have a claim on one's hospitality and assistance, and if members of one's clan rule a village one is a privileged immigrant there. Perhaps most important, the clan model serves to identify and rank *sub-clans*, the group of people in a village who are affiliated to one clan. The ranking of these groups within the village according to the clan model has significance mainly on ritual occasions. At initiation schools or at the *mokuo* (occasional communal beef-feasts) for example, members of each sub-clan are treated as a unit which is ranked relative to other sub-clans. In most secular contexts this sort of ranking is irrelevant, but some sub-clans are corporate groups which have significance in economic and political contexts. Where this is the case, the clan model helps formulate their self-image and the way in which other villagers regard them.

Kgota is a multi-referential term, but the common element in all its applications is the identification of the group referred to as patrilineally based. It may be used to refer to patrilineal categories of kin and to patrilineally recruited (or identified) local groups of various ranges. A clan or a lower level patrilineal group may be termed *kgota*, as may a sub-clan sector or a family-group site.[2]

Lošitša means 'spine' or 'seam'; and, in a social context, the category of people to whom an individual is related by active ties of kinship or affinity. The *lošitša* is conceived of as ideally a bounded group, its borders being defined by patrilineal descent from a common ancestor.

---

[1] Schapera, Krige, and other authorities prefer to talk of 'totemic groups' rather than 'clans' when writing about Sotho-speaking peoples, mainly because these groups do not have a rule of exogamy. (See, e.g., Schapera, 1953: 35; Krige, 1964: 157.) Radcliffe-Brown and others use the term 'clan' even in the absence of a rule of exogamy, however, and it seems odd to speak of totemic groups in the Southern Bantu area where totemism is of minimal importance. The Ngologa are sometimes ignorant of their totems, and disagree about the totem of the Ngologa people, while never forgetting their clan affiliation.

[2] The Ngologa do not connect *kgota* in these senses with the word for a council-place, which is also *kgota*. Nor does Brown's Tswana dictionary suggest a connection between the equivalent Tswana terms, *kgotla*. However, the Hon. Mr Q. Masire has suggested to me that there is a connection, stemming from the conception of the ruling group in a village (or a Tswana tribe) as a patrilineal corporation which 'owns' the council.

In theory, the *lošitša* is made up of intermarrying family-groups, and informants are inclined to stress the element of endogamy as the source of its solidarity and continuity. At this level of idealisation it is difficult to differentiate the *lošitša* and the *kgota*, but while recognising the difficulty informants usually insist that there is a difference.

They agree, however, that there are no groups today which correspond to the ideal *lošitša*. It existed in the recent past, but was destroyed by a rapid increase in marriages outside the kindred. Today 'the *rrakgari* (father's sister) is lost to the *lošitša*'. (The *rrakgari* is probably picked out here since it is the alliances contracted by family-group heads which have the greatest impact on inter-group relations. Further, the full impact of these alliances is felt only in the next generation, when the affinal link becomes a relationship of matrifiliation.) My evidence indicates that the Ngologa exaggerate the decline in close-kin marriages. They probably never accounted for more than about half of all marriages, as is the case today. It is improbable that the ideal *lošitša* ever existed, or indeed that a social group constituted on such lines could operate.

The Ngologa also use *lošitša* in conversation in much the same sense as the English term the 'whole family'. They then mean an ego-centred and unique group of kin, plus affines who are often not kin. A person's *lošitša* in this sense includes the members of his *kgota* and a number of other people in addition. I would stress, however, that informants are often reluctant to specify this distinction.

The Ngologa idealisation of the kinship/residence structure of the village provides a good example of the way in which these concepts are applied. The Ngologa say that each *kgota* or *lošitša* should occupy its own cluster of compounds in one sector of the village. The senior sub-clan should occupy the easternmost sector of the village, and the other groups should be settled to the west of it, in order of seniority. The junior sub-clan should thus occupy the western extremity of the village. The family-groups within these sectors should, similarly, be laid out along an arc stretching from east to west, with the patrilineally senior group in the east. The compounds within the family-group should be sited in relation to one another according to the same principles.[1]

Not only the layout of the village but the structure of authority may be conceived of in these terms. The village is sometimes said to be

---

[1] In Ngologa thought, the east is associated with life-giving forces, and the west with inutility and death.

'owned' by a clan. The citizens of Kuli, for example, may be addressed as 'Bapebana', man of the Pebana clan, from which the headman comes. The kin-based residential groups within the village may also be represented as patrilineal political units, the pattern of settlement matching the distribution of authority, with the leading groups to the east.

III

I turn now to a sociological analysis of these kin-based local groups. There are three levels of such groups among the Ngologa. First there is the family-group, a neighbourhood unit varying in size from a single nuclear family to an association of ten or more compounds with a total population of up to perhaps fifty. The core of the family-group is formed by a set of male household heads who are recruited almost exclusively from among the sons, brothers and brothers' sons of the family-group head. Full brothers are more likely to be members of one group than brothers by different women, and family-groups rarely include both brothers of the group head and his, or his brother's, adult, married sons.

Associated with this group may be a few households occupied by unmarried or divorced female kin, usually of mature age and often with children. There may also be a few men, usually illegitimate (and so without membership of an agnatic corporation), who are affinal or matrilateral connections of the group head. I call these people *associates* of the family-group, and distinguish them from the *members* and their wives and children. The associates have no independent political base. They are usually economically dependent on the group members, but do not share their jural rights in the group estate.

The inner ring of adult male agnates, the members, form a corporation which is usually headed by the genealogically senior man, though his old age, ill health or incompetence may bring about the leadership of the next senior man. The group head has some control over the estate of the members, which includes livestock and rights in the group minors, but these rights are at the same time particularised in individuals by virtue of their roles as husbands, fathers, brothers or mother's brothers. Migrant labour and other pressures towards economic individualism are having an effect, yet the high valuation of economic cooperation and corporate control remains.

The family-group members are usually treated as a single 'personality' in legal and political affairs. This unit is represented in the village court and council by the group head, and the court may hold him responsible for the torts of members and their wives and children and also (though more rarely nowadays) their serfs. The family-group head also arbitrates when domestic disputes arise, sometimes convening on such occasions a kinship council, to which he may invite kinsmen or affines from outside the group.

Family-groups rarely survive the death of the group head, and fission also often occurs when sons of the group head or his brother have adult sons. Yet despite its regularity, fission is regarded as a deviation from the norm and it is generally accompanied by severe conflicts over authority and the disposal of property. These conflicts are sometimes perceived and expressed in a mystical idiom. There may be sorcery accusations, or troubles may be attributed simply to the evil consequences of tension between brothers.

The process of fission and the subsequent realignment of family-groups involves territorial separation and the redistribution of rights in people and in property. This is a direct threat to effective agnatic relationships, which are based on the patrilineal definition of rights in property and people, and which are ideally symbolised by a special pattern of residential alignment. In some cases agnatic connections are severed amidst mutual recriminations. Typically a man will refuse to consult his brothers about marriages he or his children may make, and will settle at a distance from them. If the dominant family-group within a wider alliance splits, agnates in related groups may be drawn into the conflict, and in the end a whole sub-clan may be divided into rival factions. This is particularly likely to happen if a headman or a sub-clan head dies.

Close agnatic relationships do sometimes survive the fission of family-groups. Marriages between close agnates, which are fairly common, may help to contain the damage, although this does not always happen. Then the new family-groups—or at least some of them—will site their homes alongside each other and maintain their former relationships in a reduced form. The junior group may consult the head of the senior group about marriages, minors, cattle, and political relationships. Such family-group alliances constitute the second level of kin-based local units. They may also be formed, though less commonly, with closely related agnates who were not within the original family-group.

Although members of a family-group alliance may have close day-to-day contacts, collaborate politically, perhaps share a well, they are not as integrated as members of a family-group, unless it is on the brink of fission.

Sub-clans (as I mentioned earlier) are sometimes divided, and the members of one clan who live in a particular village may have only a categorical and ritual unity. But there are usually some solidary sub-clans which occupy a distinct sector of the village and form economic and political and administrative units. Such solidary sub-clans form the third level of kin-based local groups. Their structure is similar to that of family-groups and family-group alliances. They form about an agnatic core, in this case closely-related family-group heads, and include a periphery of groups attached by ties of kinship and affinity or by more casual ties. The patrilineal core is isolated in some ritual contexts, but in most social situations the more fluidly defined group operates.

When sub-clans split following conflicts within the core group, the factions which result are again structured about an agnatic core. From certain points of view they are indistinguishable from family-group alliances. Their peculiarity lies in the tension which exists between closely-related factions, and in the fact that there is no justification for them in Ngologa ideology. Their existence conflicts with the notions of kinship solidarity which provide a charter for political combination. Although they are of central importance in village politics, citizens sometimes deny knowledge of them.

I have been stressing the agnatic base of these social groups, and while this is by no means the whole story it may be useful to illustrate in a simple diagram the structures I have described so far (Fig. 1).

If this hypothetical sub-clan split into factions, which it might well

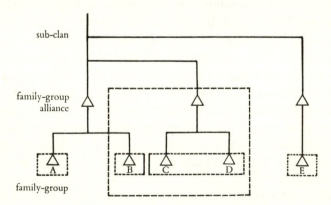

Fig. 1. Ngologa kin-based groupings.

do if A was a headman and died leaving several sons, some sons might form a faction with B, say, while the others could form an opposition in combination with C and D, E perhaps remaining neutral.

Despite the importance of agnation, descent does not mechanically determine group structure. One cannot deduce alignments through the study of family trees. Nor are the various groups frozen into postures of cooperation or opposition. The primary alignments of individuals and groups are balanced by cross-cutting ties of kinship and affinity, and some men shift their allegiances for idiosyncratic reasons. A major source of this flexibility is the importance of ties through women.

Affinal ties tend to be of less lasting importance than matrilateral ties, partly because Ngologa marriage is highly unstable[1] while the allocation of rights in children is rigid. There are exceptions. In Kuli two active members of the Silebe sub-clan are attached to it as a function of their marriages to sisters of core-group men. This is one of the exceptions that proves the rule, for they are exceptional among the village elders in having married only once each, and remaining married over the years.

Generally the relationship between sister's son and mother's brother is far more stable, in fact it is the strongest non-agnatic bond in Ngologa society. It is characterised by warmth and mutual concern, and, as Casalis noted among the Basuto over a century ago, it acts as 'a counterbalance to the authority of the father and the eldest son' (1861: 181). Moreover, the mother's brother provides an external point of reference for the matrifocal sibling group, perhaps the most cohesive unit in the society. The relationship is therefore potentially divisive from the point of view of the agnatic group, and it may even provide a lever which can be used in intra-group conflicts. Because it is free of the difficulties which bedevil agnatic relationships, and because it has strategic value in struggles for property and power between agnates, the mother's brother/sister's son relationship has obvious political potential. To quote Schapera (who was writing of the Tswana), the mother's brother 'differs markedly from a father's brother or other agnate in that he need never be feared as a possible rival for either property or position; and, on the other hand, he himself stands to benefit materially

---

[1] In a sample of thirty-two Kuli men who had between them contracted a total of sixty-eight marriages, I found that 47 per cent of marriages had ended in divorce or separation. (Twenty-eight of the marriages were still extant, and eight had been terminated by the wife's death.) Separation was common, but divorce—the formal withdrawal of all rights in women and children and the return of marriage prestations—was rare. There were thirty cases of separation and only two of divorce.

if his nephew becomes a man of wealth or the head of a large social group'. (1963: 171.)

This then, in outline, is the way in which the Ngologa view these kin-based local groups and the way in which they appear to the anthropologist. The following section deals with the development of the contemporary social groups in Kuli village.

IV

Kuli was founded in the second decade of the twentieth century by members of the Pebana clan. They came from Lehututu under the leadership of Leswape I, who had recently resigned the headmanship of that village. Leswape I had wished to step down in favour of his eldest son, Molede, but in the event Molede's claim failed. This was evidently because his mother was an outsider, perhaps of Bushman extraction. In any case he did not make a strong bid for the succession, and Leswape's second son Montsiwe, whose mother was well-connected, became the headman.

Molede and Leswape I moved to the nearby hamlet of Monong, which Molede still rules today. The water supply at Monong is very poor, however, and Leswape soon moved with several adherents to the west, finally settling in Kuli where they found sweet water and good grazing. Among the adult men who accompanied Leswape were four of his sons, Ramošwane, Riphoni, Mabote and Mokgetise; two sons of Molede, Haukgwetse and Haudwelwe; and two sons of a younger brother, Mokoenyane and Tsenene. Shortly after establishing himself in Kuli, Leswape sent for Ramaseri, the son of another younger brother, to come to the village as a London Missionary Society evangelist. The following genealogy (Fig. 2) sketches the three-generation patrilineage from which these migrants were recruited.

Other men from Lehututu accompanied this core group or joined them subsequently. Later, migrants came to Kuli from other parts of the Kalahari. An early recruit was a man named Maayane, of the Rakile clan, who was an affinal connection of Leswape's and a sort of client of his. He became one of Leswape's counsellors, but left Kuli soon after his death. One of Leswape's younger brothers joined the village briefly and left his son behind when he returned to Lehututu. He died shortly afterwards, and his son Molatesi remained in Kuli. A large Rakile group arrived from a hamlet near Lehututu. The Rakile are an off-shoot of the Pebana, and this group traces a common patrilineal ancestor with Leswape three generations back. The group included three brothers, two of whom still live together with the son of the third (deceased) brother in one family-group. They are treated as Pebana for ritual purposes, and have aligned themselves with the ruling group. More recently other small groups which have come to Kuli have attached themselves to the *BoLeswape* on the basis of some tie of kinship or affinity.

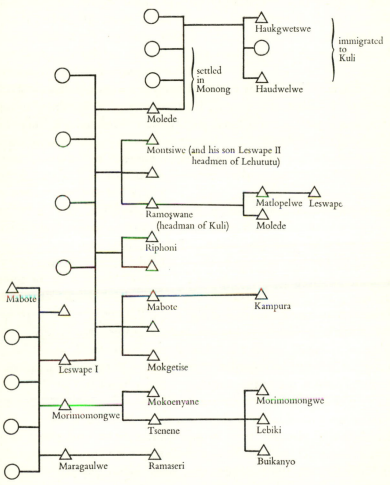

Fig. 2. The 'Sons of Leswape'.

This diverse group constitutes the Pebana sub-clan. Most of its members are treated as Pebana for ritual purposes, and they are referred to collectively as BaPebana. They are regarded as the owners or rulers (*benyi*) of Kuli. The core group, the 'Sons of Leswape', is sometimes distinguished, and for some time was a coherent co-residential unit. Intermarriage was common between the families in this group, and between them and other members of the sub-clan.

Shortly after Leswape I and his followers had established themselves in Kuli, another group arrived and formed a second sub-clan in the village, the Silebe sub-clan. (The Silebe clan is generally regarded as being allied with the Pebana.) Led by a man named Marigwe, this Silebe group had spent some time in South West Africa and then in Karakobis. It included Marigwe's son Masime and the sons of two of Marigwe's brothers, Mothibakgomo, the son of his deceased elder brother, and Modjathoši, the son of a younger brother. Marigwe's group was accompanied by a man named Mokgethi, a Pebana distantly related to the 'Sons of Leswape'. He was married to Mothibakgomo's sister, and lived (and still lives) uxorilocally. Mokgethi is fully integrated into the Silebe sub-clan, indeed he is a leading figure in it, but he is still identified as a Pebana in some ritual contexts and in conversation.

Three other immigrants have married women of the Marigwe group. Two of them, Moloise and Sebe, are Silebe but do not claim close consanguineal ties with the core Silebe group in Kuli. Sebe has become an integrated member of the sub-clan, but Moloise quarrelled with the *BoMarigwe* and now lives among Pebana, near the headman. The third man, Tšekwe, belongs to the small Kgala clan. He lives near the main Silebe complex and in general identifies himself with the Silebe.

Finally, another member of the core Silebe group, Tatawane, settled recently in Kuli. He and the other BaMarigwe, the patrilineal core of the Kuli Silebe, are sometimes distinguished as a group, like the 'Sons of Leswape'. In other contexts all the members of the Silebe clan in the village may be regarded as one group. In the normal course of events, however, the active neighbourhood alliance is treated as a unit, and its members are known as the BaSilebe.

There are in addition a few men who have never been closely identified with either of these groups. In one or two cases they play a prominent part in village affairs as independents. They may lack close kinship ties with other villages, and some belong to clans otherwise unrepresented in Kuli.

Leswape I died in the early 1940s, and within a year his family-group had split and the Pebana were divided into two opposed factions. Leswape's family-group had included his sons Ramošwane, Riphoni, Mabote and Mokgetise (the latter two sons of one woman), and his younger brother's sons Tsenene and Ramaseri. The sons of Molede,

Leswape's eldest son, formed their own family-group. It was allied to Leswape's, and in a fashion subordinate to him. (For example, when the brothers, Haukgwetse and Haudwelwe quarrelled, Leswape intervened and made the younger but more responsible Haudwelwe group head.) The remaining member of the core Pebana group, Mokoenyane, the elder brother of Tsenene, proved a restless, careless man, and was seldom in the village for any length of time.

In the year of Leswape's death Mabote left the family-group and went to live beside his field, about a quarter of a mile from his brothers. Tsenene, who was married to a full sister of Mabote, followed soon after and settled near him. Presently Mabote's full brother Mokgetise joined him. Mokoenyane's wife settled nearby, and when Mokoenyane at last settled down in Kuli he moved in with her. The family-groups of Mabote (in which Mokgetise lives), Tsenene and Mokeonyane are still neighbours and constitute a family-group alliance. This alliance is the basis of a faction which is generally opposed to the new headman, Ramošwane.

Ramošwane himself moved to the south of the village and formed his own family-group. His younger brother Riphoni formed a family-group to the west of him, and Haudwelwe brought his group to the north of Ramošwane's. These family-groups constitute an alliance which is the basis of the headman's faction. Ramaseri and a few others are more loosely attached to this faction.

During my first tour in the Kalahari, the Kuli Silebe formed an effective sub-clan in marked contrast to the feuding Pebana. There was, however, an undercurrent of conflict between Masime, who had led the group for some years, and Mothibakgomo, the son of his elder brother, who reached maturity and took over in the early sixties. When I returned to Kuli at the end of 1966, I found Mothibakgomo and other members of the group living near new fields, about three miles west of the main Silebe settlement. Masime and another member of the group had remained behind. While this seemed to indicate the early stages of fission, the ideology of agnatic unity masked the extent of the conflict. It is possible that the old residential unit was re-established after the harvest in 1967.

v

I have already touched on the importance of ties through women, which are expected to entail collaboration on a wide social front. Although they sometimes fail to achieve this, failure is regarded as abnormal and culpable. These ties may form the basis of economic cooperation, co-residence, and political alliance. Within agnatic groups they create particularly tightly-knit segments and trace the lines along which fission may take place. In discussing the development of the social groups in Kuli several examples of these effects have cropped up.

Since relationships through women are of such far-reaching importance, marriage strategies are highly significant in Ngologa social life. The ideal is that one should marry within the *lošitša*. A matrilateral cross-cousin is usually said to be the perfect choice for a man, followed by a patrilateral cross-cousin and parallel cousins. In practice, close-kin marriages[1] are common, particularly between the descendants of half-siblings. However, members of ruling sub-clans prefer to marry within the ruling group, and so tend to marry agnates, while members of subordinate groups attempt rather to build up useful alliances, and prefer marriages with non-agnates.

Of sixty-eight Kuli marriages which I recorded, nearly half (thirty-two) were with close-kin. The 'Sons of Leswape' married a higher proportion of close-kin than did other villages, and they showed a marked preference for marriages with agnates, while other villagers preferred to marry non-agnatic relatives. With a single exception, all the 'Sons of Leswape' whom I interviewed had married at least one close agnate. Of thirty-eight marriages contracted by 'Sons of Leswape', 45 per cent were with agnates, and 11 per cent with other close-kin. The thirty marriages contracted by other villagers included 13 per cent with agnates and 23 per cent with other close-kin.

The 'Sons of Leswape' are closely related by descent to the rulers of Lehututu and Monong, and some of their close agnatic marriages were with members of these groups. While I was in Kuli, a granddaughter of the headman was sent to marry a son of the Lehututu headman (her father's father's older brother's son's son), 120-odd miles away. Such 'dynastic' alliances are often of great practical value and warrant constant reinforcement through new marriages. (For instance, the previous headman of Lehututu made a gift of over £100 to the Kuli headman when the latter was raising money for a village borehole.) Within the village, agnatic marriages reinforce the solidarity of the

---

[1] By 'close-kin' I mean people related by descent from a common ancestor who is a great-grandparent of one or both of the parties, or a closer ancestor. This usage is based on Schapera's (see Schapera, 1950: 158 and 1957: 140). In general my thinking on the implications of Ngologa close-kin marriage is strongly influenced by Schapera's work on similar Tswana kinship marriages. See Schapera, 1950; 1957; and 1963 (*a*) and (*b*).

ruling set, secure participation in power for its members, and maintain the communication of support to the headman. As I have said, these advantages do not accrue automatically, and in Kuli the split of the Pebana sub-clan ruptured a number of alliances.

The aim of subordinate groups (by which I mean here groups outside the descent group which founded Kuli), is to seek security through alliances with the ruling group in their own or other villages. Secession and migration are seen as perennial options, and therefore connections with powerful groups in other villages are highly valued. Their marriages show a wide geographical spread. The significance of such choices is clear to the people. When I suggested to a Silebe elder in Kuli that his clan was powerless since it did not rule any villages, he countered: 'We are headmen in our own right. We are the parents of all the people in the Kalahari. *The Silebe and their sisters' children are everywhere!'*

Ties through women are perhaps of even greater importance for villagers outside the major agnatic groupings. I have already cited the case of the two elders who are allied to the Silebe only through their marriages to two sisters of core group members, and who are so exceptional as not to have separated from their wives. They are important for everyone, however, and to underline the significance of such relationships, and the interaction of marriage choices and political events, I present two brief case studies.

A. *Molateši*

Molateši could claim to be a member of Leswape I's patrilineage, and, in addition, an affinal and matrilateral connection, as Fig. 3 shows.

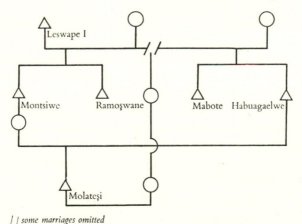

| | some marriages omitted

Fig. 3. Molateši's alliances with the 'Sons of Leswape'.

Molateši's father had died while on a visit to Lehututu and his mother had gone off with another man. Molateši grew up in Mabote's home, but since his father had not paid *bogari* (the main bridewealth payment, which legitimises children), he could not be a full member of Mabote's group unless Mabote chose to pay the *bogari* himself, or Molateši managed to raise the price on his own. In strict legal terms he belonged to the mother's people, represented in Kuli by Ramošwane. Nevertheless he worked as a herdsman for Mabote until he had grown up, sometimes staying at distant cattle-posts at Kalkfontein and Makunda.

In 1948 Molateši went to South West Africa in search of cash labour, and for twelve years he worked on various Afrikaans farms. On his return to Kuli he built a compound in Ramošwane's part of the village. He now lives, he says, among his *bomalone*, his mother's agnates.

He explains his choice as follows: he stayed with Mabote initially and worked for him because Mabote had no sons. But since Mabote has not paid *bogari* he is not his 'son', and Mabote now has five sons of his own. He finds it preferable to live among his mother's people under the present circumstances, but adds that after Mabote's death he will pay his mother's *bogari* himself. This will give him a secure position in the village as one of the 'Sons of Leswape' without involving him with Mabote against Ramošwane.

B. *Waatotsi*

Waatotsi's mother was a full sister of headman Ramošwane of Kuli. After his birth his mother married a man named Piti, who paid the *bogari* and became Waatotsi's legal father.

Waatotsi and his powerful mother's brother, Ramošwane, furthered their relationship by intermarriage. Waatotsi married the daughter of a half-sister of Ramošwane (his own mother's sister's daughter), and Ramošwane married a half-sister of his. Waatotsi and his family also intermarried with other families among the 'Sons of Leswape'.

Watotsi grew up in Matšeng. His mother separated from Piti, however, and since Piti was not his biological father, Waatotsi's status in his group was not, perhaps, completely comfortable. He migrated to Ukwi when he reached maturity, and then left Ukwi for Nojane and Nojane for Kuli. He told me:

I came from Nojane, saying there are Tlharo and Rolong [i.e. Tswana] there, and therefore I came to my mother's brother (*malome*) here. I said, I am a Ngologa, my mother's brother is Ramošwane, and I do not want to pay tax to the Tlharo. I came here, and I explained to the District Commissioner that I moved because Ramoŝwane is my *malome*—like my mother. I did not waste time asking the permission of [the headman of Nojane] for he is not my mother or my father.

Waatotsi began as a supporter of headman Ramoŝwane, but later he became a political independent, and for a period in the early sixties he was generally ranged with Mabote against Ramoŝwane. This situation conflicted with the network of affinal and matrilateral ties which he had, in part, created. He reacted by hindering marriages between his family and Ramoŝwane's, and by encouraging alliances with Mabote's family.

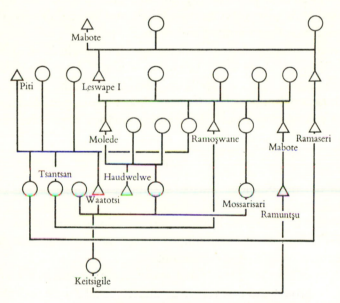

Fig. 4. Waatotsi's alliances with the 'Sons of Leswape'.

In 1961 or 1962 Ramoŝwane's eldest son's son, Leswape, came to pay *pholo* (the second bridewealth payment) for a girl to whose mother Waatotsi had once been married. Waatotsi retained some influence and demanded a steep price and, in addition, payments for alleged slights to the bride and her family. Ramoŝwane was incensed and threatened to call upon the girl's mother's brother, who, like Waatotsi, was his sister's son, to support him—thus demonstrating that expectations of support from kin connected through women can survive experiences of the contrary.

About two years later Mabote's son Ramuntšu paid *bogari* for a daughter of Waatotsi. The negotiations went without a hitch, but while all the members of Mabote's faction were present, only one member of the headman's faction attended the ceremony. This was despite their close agnatic relationship to the groom. The sole exception was Leswape, who as court-scribe attended to register the marriage payment.

Shortly after the event the headman, Ramošwane, complained to me: 'Waatotsi and Mabote did not inform me of Ramuntšu's payment. Therefore I think they are against me.' He had been slighted as Mabote's brother, as Waatotsi's mother's brother, and as village headman. The ceremony had clear political implications. The breach between Ramošwane and Mabote was further dramatised, and Waatotsi's new political orientation was demonstrated and strengthened.

However, alliances based on marriage are fraught with difficulty. Waatotsi and Mabote soon began to quarrel about details of the marriage, and at least once publicly abused each other in the village council. When I returned to Kuli in 1966 I found that Waatotsi had left and was making a visit of uncertain duration with a brother in a distant part of the country.

VI

To sum up, the Ngologa normally express the organisation of residential groups and the structure of authority in kinship terms. As I have shown there is in fact an intimate relationship between solidary kin-based groups and residential units, although the people do not provide a satisfactory analysis of the situation.

Groups within the village form about agnatic cores at three levels, the family-group, the family-group alliance (or faction) and the sub-clan. People may also be attached to these groups through more distant agnatic connections or ties through women.

Close agnatic relationships form the basis of the organisation of authority and property. They are therefore peculiarly susceptible to tensions between men. Connections through women may divide segments of these agnatic core groups and plot the lines along which new groups emerge after the fission of the old. Ties of this sort also permit men with inadequate agnatic bases of support to form alliances and establish secure and even influential positions in the network of village relationships.

In Kuli village there are two sub-clans, the Pebana and the Silebe.

5. The District Commissioner addresses the *lekgota*.
(The Kuli headman is seated facing him.)

6. A special meeting of the Kuli *lekgota*.
From left to right: the District Commissioner, the Vice-President of Botswana,
the village headman and the District Councillor.

7. The District Councillor addresses the *lekgota*.

8. Listening to a *lekgota* debate.

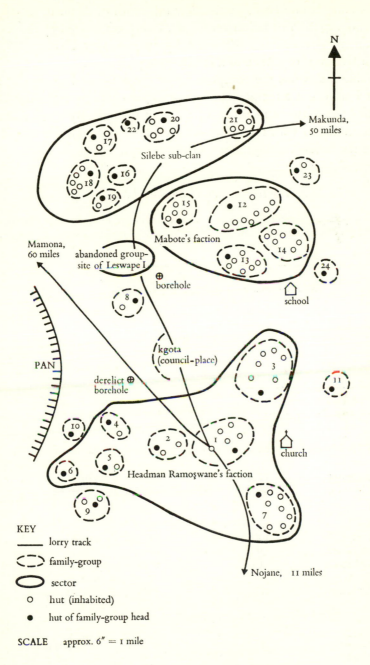

Map. 3. Sketch-map of Kuli village.

While the Silebe have remained a fairly united group, the Pebana sub-clan split into two factions after the death of its head, Leswape I, the founder and first headman of Kuli. One faction is led by the present headman, Ramoŝwane, the other by his younger brother Mabote. Each faction is organised as a family-group alliance.

Table 2 sets out the composition of the kin-based groups in Kuli (but I have not attempted to compress into tabular form the cross-cutting ties between members of different groups). By using this table in conjunction with the sketch-map of Kuli (Map 3), the reader can trace the residential alignments of the groups.

Table 2. *The composition of kin-based local groups in Kuli*

(I present kinship relationships in abbreviated form, using only the first two letters of each kinship term. The letters 'o' and 'y' signify older and younger. Thus FayBrSo = father's younger brother's son.)

	FAMILY-GROUP			CLAN	FACTION
No.*	Name of head	Size†	Relationship of members to head‡	Clan of head	Relationship to faction head Comments

A. THE FACTION OF RAMOŜWANE, HEADMAN OF KULI

(1) Closely-involved members of the faction

1. § Ramoŝwane	22	2So SoSo	Pebana	Faction head
2. § Riphoni	17	So	Pebana	yBr
3. § Haudwelwe	46	oBr	Pebana	oBrSo

(2) Less closely-attached member of the faction

4. § Ramaseri	10(?)	So	Pebana	FayBrSo
5. Mojakake	3(?)	So	Pebana	Distant connection
6. § Molateŝi	4	—	Pebana	oBrDaSo; also yBrSo. (See case-study A above.)
7. Monantwe	32	2So oBr oBrSo yBrSo	Rakile	Distant agnate
8. § Molede	8	—	Pebana	Ramoŝwane's son by wife dismissed for sorcery. Lives with mother

B. UNAFFILIATED GROUPS IN THE SOUTH OF KULI

9. Waatotsi	12	2So	Pebana	(See case-study B above.)
10. Moloise	3	—	Silebe	Split with Kuli Silebe despite marriage bond
11. Motojwane	2(?)	—	Pebana	Brother of Lehututu headman: a recluse

C. THE FACTION OF MABOTE, THE HEADMAN'S YOUNGER BROTHER

12. § Mabote	29	So yBr yBrSo	Pebana	Faction head
13. § Tsenene	19	3So	Pebana	FayBrSo
14. § Mokoenyane	15	3So	Pebana	FayBrSo (he is Tsenene's oBr)
15. Kati	?	—	—	The only woman group head in Kuli. She was once married to Mabote but joined the group formed by her married So. On his death she became *de facto* head

D. THE SILEBE SUB-CLAN

16. § Mothibakgomo	8	—	Silebe	Sub-clan head
17. Mokgethi	12	So	Pebana	SiHu
18. § Masime	34	yBr	Silebe	FayBrSo (acted as sub-clan head until Mothibakgomo's maturity)
19. § Modjathoši	19	2yBr	Silebe	FayBrSo
20. Sebe	5	—	Silebe	Married to Masime's sister
21. Tšekwe	?	2So	Kgala	Married to Masime's sister
22. § Tatawane	8	—	Silebe	Close agnate

E. UNAFFILIATED GROUPS IN THE NORTH OF KULI

23. Mahupunyane	?	?	Ngologa	Distant ties through mother with headman, and informal ties with Silebe neighbours
24. Bogope	?	?	Rakile	New immigrant. Son of Mabote's sister, and sometimes associated with his faction

* See sketch-map of Kuli (Map 3).
† Including members, minors and associates.
‡ Excluding minors and associates.
§ Member of core agnatic group.

I have been discussing co-residential social groups which are recruited and organised, and conceived of, largely in terms of kinship. These are the most pervasive social units in the village and function in various areas of social life. Their politico–jural aspect, which will be of central concern in the following chapters, has been touched on; and here I wish briefly to comment on some of their other social and economic functions.

The family-group is a field of intense interaction and familial cooperation. A person feels at home anywhere in his family-group, and children treat the group site as their range soon after they begin to walk. I often found myself thinking of the group site as a single 'house' with many 'rooms', an essentially accurate image.

The members of the family-group generally cooperate in economic affairs, and often associates share some of the labour and rewards. Modern economic opportunities, however, foster individualism. For example, a man I knew well in Kalkfontein (a village more influenced by modern economic pressures than Kuli) was sent by a missionary society to be trained in a Rhodesian school with a view to becoming an evangelist. His father sold some property to help finance his studies, and sent my friend's younger brother along with him. After two years the brothers returned for a vacation.

We found there had been no rain. My father was an old man. The cattle were troubling him. I told him to hire a helper, but he could not find anybody who was willing to work. So it was very difficult for me to return to school. One of my brothers who had stayed at home [working as an assistant in a white-owned store] neglected the cattle.

That year there was no food. People were starving. I tried to persuade my brother who had stayed at home to help my parents, but he refused until we gave up. I told my brother that he should return to school, I would remain and look after the cattle. He said, No, you go. I will stay and look after the cattle. But I said, I have children and a wife, you would not be able to support them. My brother agreed and went back to Bulawayo. I sold an ox for R18, of which I gave him R14. I also killed a goat to provision him for his journey.

Only a nuclear family is involved here, but the pressures towards sharing goods and responsibilities apply even in larger family-groups— although resistance, particularly from cash-earners, is likely to be greater. The conflicts which may arise emerge vividly from a speech Modjathoši once made to the Kuli court (*lekgota*) about his younger brother, Thage.

While Thage was at work [as a labour migrant in South West Africa] he sent home R15. R5 was for his mother, R10 for me. We were to expect nothing further from him. I did not use this money. I sold an ox for R15. With the R25 I now had, I bought a rifle for Thage. [Later he was paid part of his army pension and used some of this money to buy a cow.] I gave this cow to Thage . . .

All these things I did for Thage. Once Thage wrote to me to ask whether his property was still all right. I did not reply. He wrote again, accusing me of having 'eaten' the money he had sent. I told him to find someone else to handle his affairs here, but he did not. Nowadays, if I go to Nojane or go out hunting, Thage destroys my property. He is like an animal, like lightning. He must be 'killed'.

The men in a family-group frequently share the job of watering livestock, even though some cattle may be individual purchases while others belong to the common herd under the control of the group head. In the same way, the group's herdboys will often work together, and the group may share a cattle-post.

The gardens are the domain of the women.[1] Individual women may have their own gardens, though sometimes the women of a group share one plot; but they combine to form work-groups recruited from within the family-group for the chores leading from sowing and weeding to harvesting. The men and boys do the ploughing, and the draught-oxen may be shared within the family-group or even the wider circle of the family-group alliance. All hands, often including Bushman serfs, are engaged in the harvest.

The family-group alliance also forms a fairly intimate social unit, and so may a sub-clan if it is small and cohesive like the Kuli Silebe. These groups are also characterised by the expectation of mutual aid, particularly in projects which require a large investment of labour or capital. House-building is one example, but more long-term cooperative units may be formed to secure water supplies. Wells may be sunk in the pan by individuals or family-groups (sometimes hiring semi-skilled artisans within the village), but often the men of a family-group alliance band together to sink a well and cooperate in watering stock. At a more sophisticated level (in Kalkfontein and elsewhere) the men in a family-group alliance may even combine to invest in a borehole, an expensive undertaking. Kuli has a borehole sunk by

[1] The main crops are melons, maize and beans. Mr George Silberbauer, for many years a government officer in Ghanzi District, estimates that on average only one harvest every three years is sufficiently successful to feed villagers without resort to the importation of cereals.

Government. At one stage those men who used it divided into two groups which bought the diesel fuel in rotation. These groups corresponded closely to the two Pebana factions. One group included Ramoŝwane, Riphoni, Haudwelwe and Monantwe, and the other included Mabote, Tsenene, Mokoenyane and, for a while, an outsider, Mahupunyane.

VIII

Some other activities in the village depend less on these kin-based local groupings, and may even divide them. Every village has more than one church. Even a small village like Kuli has both the ubiquitous London Missionary Society and an Independent church, the African Methodist Episcopalian.[1] The leaders of the congregations are usually men, and the services are led by literate men, but women are active in church communities and enjoy authority in committees. While the major factions in a village are often broadly co-extensive with particular congregations, there is usually some overlap. Also some older men who may be prominent in village affairs are not closely associated with any church. In recent years the Kalahari has been swept by several prophetic movements which reached their peak in the early years of the recent drought. These temporarily united some villages—including Kuli— in a single congregation.

Leswape I established the London Missionary Society in Kuli. After his death Mabote joined the African Methodist Episcopalian Church, and despite Ramoŝwane's opposition formed a congregation in the village. This move may not have been politically motivated: it seems that the LMS refused to accept Mabote as a member since he had several wives at the same time. However, the AME is not well-organised in Kuli, and even Mabote attends LMS services from time to time.

There are a few traditional ceremonies which include all the villagers. When an ox dies or is killed, most men in the village collect for the communal *mokuo* feast. Sometimes the women have their own feast at the same time. Most villagers also attend the ceremonies which follow the killing of a man's first lion or leopard, and again the major division is between men and women. The same applies to many dances.

---

[1] There are no missions in the Kalahari, and all the churches are run by local evangelists, some of whom receive small salaries from the mission organisation. The Independent churches (such as the AME) are also affiliated to broader southern African organisations.

More casual social events bring together like-minded villagers. If someone organises a 'tea-party' (a sort of temporary bar and cabaret), people will drop in to carouse from all over the village. Soccer games on the school playing-field bring together the young men, and the girls play netball. Young labour migrants at home between tours often band together, and, particularly in the larger villages, one sees them going from one 'tea-party' to another, ostentatiously playing urban gambling games, or swaggering outside the store.

The primary schools, which have come to all the villages since World War II, also create groups of children which cross-cut other divisions in the village. In time they may have a greater impact, as a school-educated generation comes to maturity. Already in some of the larger villages literate, English-speaking men, who have been exposed to city life, form friendship groups, which in recent years have occasionally become politically significant.

Informal groupings of men and women are particularly common among the unmarried younger people, but their traditional counter-parts, the age-sets, have fallen away. The last initiation ceremonies in the Kalahari were held shortly after World War II (just before the expansion of primary education). Although the elders often say that they would like to organise new initiation schools, they fear Government opposition and face the reluctance of the young.

The age-organisation was pan-village. It provided the work groups for community projects and contributed in several ways to the main-tenance of order. The age-sets of both men and women had a system of internal discipline and punished members who deviated from their rules or who disgraced them. Some older men attribute the drunken-ness, license and aggressiveness of many young men in Kgalagari villages today to the decline of the age-set system, although labour migration is obviously a contributory factor.

Work on communal projects is no longer carried out on an age-set basis, and young men often refuse to participate in community projects because they are prepared to work only for cash rewards. Nowadays community work forces are organised by the headman and council (*lekgota*) and are divided only into groups of men and women.

Since the village is a unit of administration, veterinary and medical officers, cattle-buyers and other outsiders approach the villagers as a single group. And because they are treated as a group, the villagers organise a communal front in various administrative and commercial situations. For example, the village men have built a special kraal to which they bring their stock when the cattle-guard (a veterinary department officer) wishes to enumerate or innoculate them. They also gather here with stock they wish to sell when a buyer comes to the village from Ghanzi or from further abroad. In Kuli, the headman's son may be called on to do the bargaining for all the sellers, assisted by one of his younger brothers who speaks Afrikaans.

This rapid survey indicates how few intra-village groupings cross-cut the multi-purpose kin-based local groups. Moreover, most activity at community level is a function of the administrative and political structure—the village is a political community. Consequently the daily life of the adult men is organised in terms of a dichotomy between the domestic and the politico–jural domains of social action. This is not to say that these domains are discrete; simply, they are governed by different conditions. As I have already shown, domestic events and strategies may have political consequences, and there is also a feed-back from the political to the domestic sphere.

IX

Most Kalahari villages contain pockets of foreign communities in addition to the locally dominant ethnic groups. With the exception of the Bushmen, these minorities follow a way of life similar to that of the Kgalagari; and, with the further exception of the small Nama Hottentot groups, they are culturally cognate. Their position in Kgalagari or Tswana-ruled villages is rather like that of a subordinate sub-clan, although they are generally more self-contained. Kgalagari groups in Tswana villages and Tswana groups in Kgalagari villages are the most integrated, while Herero minorities are less involved in community affairs, and the Hottentots tend to form hamlets cut off from the mainstream of village life. The position of the Bushmen is very different from that of the other minorities, however, and they require special attention.[1]

Bushmen who live around Kalahari villages are usually serfs of Bantu masters. Serfdom is traditional in Botswana. The Kgalagari were themselves once serfs of Tswana masters, and there are still Bushmen ('Sarwa') 'owned' by Bantu masters all over the country, and particularly in the west.

[1] In investigating and analysing the master-serf relationship, I was greatly assisted by Mr G. B. Silberbauer, then Bushman Survey officer of the Bechuanaland Government. We collaborated on a paper on this subject, which appeared in *African Studies* (1966).

A number of Kgalagari in western Botswana own serfs, and a few men, usually headmen, have large bands of serfs. These Bushmen serfs sometimes live on the periphery of villages, and may cultivate gardens and raise stock in addition to more traditional hunting and gathering activities. Nevertheless, their way of life still presents a marked contrast to that of the Kgalagari, a contrast which the Kgalagari express in their comments that the Bushmen live like wild animals, without leaders, without permanent villages, and without law.

There are two main Bushmen groups attached to Kuli: the Lala, who are settled to the south-west of the village, and the Nharo, who live in the north-east. The Lala (said to be products of Kgalagari-Bushmen interbreeding) speak a southern Bushman language. Their master is Ramošwane, the headman, whose father Leswape I brought them with him to Kuli when he came from Lehututu. The Nharo, who belong to the Central group of Bushmen, are attached to the Kuli Silebe. Mothibakgomo, the Silebe head, inherited some from his father's brother. The rest he controls on behalf of the headman of Kalkfontein, their master and his matrilateral kinsman. A few Nharo were taken over by Mahupunyane, another villager, in piratical fashion. One of them revolted against his treatment and placed himself under the protection of another villager, who is now regarded as his master.

A few of the serfs live with their masters in the village, but most of them live in the settlements on the outskirts of Kuli. The 'domestic serf' has a more intimate relationship with his master than does the 'outside serf', but even he may be permitted to leave his master for periods of hunting and gathering in the bush, or for a stretch of migrant labour.

The domestic serfs assist in work about the house and participate in domestic chores. The work of the outside serfs is seasonal and less well-defined. In the past they had to pay a tribute to their masters in the form of meat, skins, honey and wild fruits, and they were expected to be at their masters' disposal for certain duties. Tribute is no longer exacted, although Bushmen are still expected to make seasonal presentations of berries, skins, etc., in return for tobacco and other goods. There is normally little compulsion involved. The serfs still come into the village to fulfil seasonal demands for labour, and in return are housed and fed. Other services provided by the Bushmen include the magical treatment of illnesses and dancing for rain.

A Ngologa will describe himself as the *munyi* of a serf. This term is usually translated 'owner' in dictionaries of Sotho languages, but as Gluckman has remarked for the Lozi, 'Any position in any social relationship may be described as ownership, depending on whose rights to demand the fulfilment of obligations are being emphasised. Dominantly, the senior in the relationship is called owner' (1965: 163). The superior in an asymmetric kinship relationship may be termed *munyi*, and the Ngologa do often use kinship models to describe their relationship with their serfs. The serfs are the 'younger brothers' or 'sons' of the master. Despite this (literally) paternalistic imagery, the serfs are not protected by the sanctions inherent in the kinship system, and they do not have the rights of kin.

Moreover, the Ngologa look down on the Bushmen as inferiors. This attitude is not strictly speaking a racist one. They regard the linguistically and racially cognate Hottentots as 'ordinary people' (*bathyo heri*) and treat them as equals. Their attitude to the Bushmen derives rather from socio–economic considerations. The Hottentots, like the Ngologa and most of the people of Botswana, are cattle-keepers. They are therefore more acceptable. The semi-nomadic, apparently anarchic Bushmen still present a marked contrast economically and socially to the Ngologa. A further factor which must condition their attitudes is that while the Hottentots frequently defeated Ngologa groups in battle, the Bushmen apparently submitted to them without difficulty.

The economic contrasts between Ngologa and Bushmen not only reinforce the Ngologa conviction that the Bushmen are inferior, poor creatures: they also provide the *raison d'être* for the institution of serfdom. The economic differences make the exchange of goods and services seem worthwhile to both parties, and the master-serf relationship allows the organisation of these exchanges. The Ngologa command a less uncertain source of water than the Bushmen, and they can provide foods not found in the wild, and, above all, tobacco. In return for a share in these assets, the Bushmen provide veld-foods, game meats and skins, peculiar skills such as their tracking expertise, and occasional labour.

The jural position of the Bushmen is ill-defined nowadays, for various circumstances are bringing about an improvement in their status. However, they do not in practice enjoy the protection of the village courts unless they can interest a Government official in their case or unless their master is prepared to move on their behalf. The master is still theoretically responsible for the torts of a serf. Politically the Bushmen have no power whatsoever within the framework of village politics, and they do not attend regular sessions of the village assembly (*lekgota*).

Bushman serfs are still inherited or given as dowry, but they are no longer bought outright. The Ngologa argue that serfs are not a sound investment, for one has no redress if a serf runs away or spends long years as a labour migrant in Ghanzi or South West Africa. (And in any case, as an informant pointed out, one can eat a dead ox, but a serf's usefulness comes to an end when he dies.)

Three main factors are bringing about a change in the status of Bushmen serfs in the Kalahari. The first is labour migration, an escape route and a means of earning goods which make the serf less dependent on his master. Serfs are supposed to hand over their earnings to their masters, but usually only a nominal payment is made.

Secondly, in the last years of the colonial era Government began to take a more active interest in the treatment of Bushmen. Complaints of ill-usage made by Bushmen to the police have been dealt with, and in several cases headmen have been instructed to hear particular cases brought by Bushmen. The result is that Bushmen are now protected to a greater degree from the whims of their masters. They were not maltreated as a rule in the past, but there is now more security against the occasional unscrupulous master. The Ngologa complain that Bushmen are now 'owned by Government' and cannot be punished for their misdeeds—but police help them find and punish Bushmen driven to stock-theft in hungry seasons.

Thirdly, the Democratic Party has urged that Bushmen should be better treated in the new Botswana. Racial distinctions are being abolished, everyone is now equal before the law, and Bushmen must become ordinary and equal members of the new nation which is being formed in Botswana. This line of reasoning has had a certain impact in the Kalahari villages.

Although the institution of serfdom has been modified, it will not disappear until the economic status of the Bushmen is revolutionised. Today the communities of masters and of serfs still exist. Their relationship has not necessitated far-reaching social or cultural adjustments on the part of either group. Some Ngologa speak a Bushman language, and most male serfs speak Ngologa. Serf Bushman villages are more stable than those of the hunters and gatherers, and some serfs practise a marginal husbandry, but the band organisation has remained intact. There is little contact between serfs from different Bushman groups.

Most significantly, while some Ngologa men take Bushman concubines, I have not come across any case of Ngologa–Bushman marriage. The Ngologa may invoke the kinship model to describe their relationship with their serfs, but there are no kinship ties between them and the Bushmen. Finally, if one views the village as a politico–jural community, the Bushmen are perpetual minors.

3

THE DISTRICT ADMINISTRATION
AND THE 'NEW MEN'

I

Kalahari villages have always been isolated. Clanship provided—and still provides—a framework within which inter-village action is possible, but it has seldom been used for political purposes. The sheer distance between clan-related ruling houses has prevented the formation of effective federal units on this basis, and neighbouring villages are ruled by members of different clans. In any case, village authorities find it difficult enough to control one village, and there seems to be no desire to federate. Even hamlets which are formally under the hegemony of a metropolitan village may effectively run their own affairs, particularly if—like Ohe and Monong, for example—they are a day's journey from the metropolis.

The intrusion of the colonial regime confirmed this situation. It will be remembered that Kuli and a few other settlements were founded by a headman of Lehututu, Leswape I. When I asked the present headman of Lehututu, Leswape II, whether he still 'owned' Kuli, he said,

No. Long ago, in the days of my grandfather, Leswape ruled from Kuli and Ukwi to here. But then Government created Ghanzi District. We asked Government where our people in Ghanzi would pay tax. Government said that while they would pay in Ghanzi, a percentage would be returned to Lehututu for the Tribal Treasury. This was not done. They took Kuli, Nojane and Ukwi for Ghanzi District. We gave up.

The people of Kuli sometimes claim rights over Nojane—they say that since Leswape I owned Nojane the people of that village should pay their tax through the Kuli headman. They are aware, however, that neither Government nor the Nojane authorities will agree. This must be seen rather as an attempt to assert Ngologa primacy in the District, a long-standing if rather idle aim which was briefly significant in the period leading up to Botswana's Independence.

The establishment of the District Administration served to redefine the independence of the villages of each other and to create an over-arching administrative structure which embraced them all. Modern

Kalahari village politics must be studied in the context of the local government system, but in contrast to most systems of local government in industrialised countries, the base is structured in terms foreign to the rest of the system. In Weberian language, the base is traditional, the superstructure bureaucratic. Moreover, the two levels are not well integrated. One sees contradictions in values, failures in communication and divergences in modes of organisation. Nevertheless these two levels are integrally connected.

II

A British Protectorate was established in Bechuanaland in 1885 with the qualified consent of the major Tswana chiefs. Understandably nervous about Boer intentions, the chiefs accepted British control over vast areas of land including most of the Kalahari. As Hailey observes, however, 'What the chiefs were offering could better be described as their "spheres of influence" than as their tribal lands' (1953: 194). On their side the British declared the Protectorate with some reluctance. The High Commissioner stressed at the outset the limited responsibility envisaged:

We have no interest in the country to the north of the Molopo, except as a road to the interior; we might therefore confine ourselves for the present to preventing that part of the Protectorate being occupied by either filibusters or foreign Power, doing as little in the way of administration or settlement as possible.[1]

With the negotiation of the South African Union in 1909 it was agreed that the High Commission territories (including Bechuanaland) would in due course be handed over to South Africa. This confirmed the British in their apathy, and for the next generation the country was allowed to stagnate.

Informed radical commentators in the thirties were scathing. Barnes remarked that, 'The British came into the Bechuana country to keep the Boers out, and they have ever since been inclined to suppose that in safeguarding the Bechuana peoples from outside aggression—Afrikaner on south and east, German on west—their duty has been done'. And he concluded that: 'today the Bechuana are probably poorer and certainly less congenially governed than at any time during the last thirty years' (1932: 191–2). The Ballingers reached similar conclusions, and the general condemnation was repeated in more guarded terms by

[1] Cited by Sillery, 1952: 96.

Sir Alan Pim, who compiled a report for the British Government in 1933.[1]

The Pim Report heralded a general re-orientation of Government policy in the Protectorate. The Proclamations of 1934 marked a new concern with administration, and some 'development' was initiated. Further legislation, in 1943, settled the Protectorate's local government system for the following twenty years.[2]

The Kalahari Districts, which were defined as Crown Lands in contrast to the Tswana Reserves in the east, were even more neglected than the rest of the country. The peoples of the Kalahari were probably unaware that they were 'protected persons of the crown' until a group of European farmers under a British officer established a settlement at Ghanzi in 1898. The officer-in-charge displaced some Kgalagari from the new Ghanzi ranching area, and in due course two police posts were established. For a long time the European ranching community gave the area the only importance it had in the eyes of Government. This emerges clearly, for example, from the comment of Sillery (a former Resident Commissioner) that, 'though settlements had long been established at Ghanzi in the west, and the eastern areas contained the bulk of the population of the Protectorate, the forbidding and waterless area in between was still the untouched haunt of untamed Bushmen [sic]' (1958:98). The context shows that he is referring to the *European* settlements at Ghanzi. The fact that over 20,000 semi-pastoral Bantu and 'tamed' Bushmen inhabited the 'forbidding and waterless area in between' was often ignored at the capital and played down in the District headquarters. There were even long periods in the post-war decades when either or both of the vast Kalahari Districts were left without any District Officers and administered by remote control from Maun or Lobatsi.

The European settlers had been given to understand that Ghanzi District would be kept clear of African farmers, but Bantu settlements flourished in the south and west of the District, and new settlements were formed. Although the Africans were allowed to occupy their lands (once the farming area around Ghanzi had been cleared), little attempt was made at first to administer the villages in the area. For

[1] See *Britain in Southern Africa (No. 2): Bechuanaland Protectorate*, by Margaret L. Hodgson and W. G. Ballinger (1931). Sir Alan Pim's *Financial and Economic Position of the Bechuanaland Protectorate* was published by H.M.S.O. in 1933.
[2] The administrative implications of the Pim Report, and the Native Administration Proclamations of 1934 and 1943, are discussed in Hailey, 1953: 210–28. A rather smug review of Government policy and achievements in this period is given in Sillery, 1952: 96–103.

some time the visits of police officers and administrative personnel to villages in the Kalahari Crown Lands were incidents on hunting and exploring safaris rather than part of a planned attempt to impose effective British hegemony. These officers contented themselves with the extortion of taxes, the punishment of undutiful behaviour to Europeans, and sporadic and arbitrary intervention in local political disputes. This ended in the 1930s, and is still regarded nostalgically by some Europeans as a golden age of adventure and enterprise.[1]

However, the thirties mark an epoch even in the Kalahari. For the first time lorries began regularly to cross the country, and the development of South West Africa by the South African Government created new and relatively accessible markets for labour and stock for the people in Ghanzi District. The people of Matšeng began to travel to the Witwatersrand to work on the gold-mines. Particularly in the late 1940s, schools were set up in Kalahari villages, boreholes sunk, and medical and veterinary services initiated. At the same time the local government system was overhauled.

In the large Tswana Reserves of eastern Botswana, administration was carried on by the District Commissioners in partnership with powerful chiefs. In the Kalahari there were no important traditional rulers but merely a set of petty headmen, and a rather different form of administration had to be devised. Essentially the District Commissioner was given complete control, though his power was limited in practice by inadequate communications—in every sense of the word. The peculiar position of these District Commissioners was recognised in the 1950s, when they were designated African Authorities. They were expected to combine many of the functions of the Tswana chief with those of the British administrator.

Despite the increasing systematisation of Kalahari District administration in the post-war years, it never achieved a high level of efficiency. There were serious obstacles in the way of what the British considered good administration. The worst problem was probably the poverty of communications. With the exception of a small police-post at Tshane, manned by African personnel, administrative and police officers were stationed in European and Coloured farming areas. From these 'camps' the officials toured the villages every month or two, seldom spending more than a few hours in each. (The villages are visited by District Commissioners, police, veterinary and medical personnel and school inspectors. On a rough average, a village is visited by one or two officials

[1] Hodson, a police officer, captures this era in his memoirs, *Trekking the Great Thirst* (1912).

every month.) Until and even after Independence, most of the high-level officials were European. Many of them were ignorant of the various local languages and depended on interpreters, who were not always satisfactory.[1] In the long intervals between their visits, the District officials kept in touch with the village authorities by letter, normally writing in English. This was not conducive to ready communication. Posts were slow and unreliable, and few villagers are literate—hardly anyone is educated beyond Standard VI.

There were other problems as well. One was the rapid turnover of high-level personnel, and their ignorance of the culture and social organisation of the people they ruled. Another was the poverty of the resources at their command. The Bechuanaland Protectorate Government was chronically understaffed and poorly financed, and the Kalahari Districts were low on the order of priorities.

Under these circumstances, the District Commissioner depended on the cooperation of the villagers if his projects were to succeed, and the village political community enjoyed a certain autonomy. But the villages were not economically self-sufficient, and the power of the District Commissioner, though limited by the obstacles I have mentioned, was recognised by the villagers and even exaggerated. Consequently there was considerable mutual accommodation.

Regular supervision of the village courts and headmen was extremely difficult to achieve, and the villagers were often able to manoeuvre the District authorities into doing (or not doing) something, the consequences of which they did not appreciate. However, the District Administration was fairly successful in the field of welfare, given the limited resources available. In the twenty years preceding Botswana's Independence (in 1966), schools and boreholes were provided in all Kalahari villages, skeleton veterinary and medical services set up, and famine relief organised in years of severe drought. These services were established with the full cooperation of the villagers, who raised funds and helped operate them.

In short, Kalahari District Administration was a formal autocracy leavened in practice by poor communications. Until the period of reform in the mid-1960s, the only move to delegate important functions

---

[1] I attended several meetings which a particular District Commissioner called in Kuli in 1964. His Tswana interpreter despised the Ngologa, and although he spoke their language he insisted on translating from English into Tswana, a second language to his auditors, whom he was in any case gratuitously insulting. The villagers repeatedly complained about this to the District Commissioner, but he failed to take the point that there are real differences between SeTswana and ŠiKgalagari.

of the District Commissioner was the appointment in 1953 of the Hukuntsi headman as sub-chief of the villages in Northern Kgalagadi District. The new sub-chief headed a court of appeal from the village courts and was also given control of a Tribal Treasury for Northern Kgalagadi and a small civil service. A police-post at nearby Tshane was instructed to give him full support, and he became as autocratic if perhaps more in touch—and more partisan—than the District Commissioner. He enjoyed the great advantages of long tenure of office and ready communication with the people under his control, but his growing disinclination for traditional democratic forms gradually alienated a large group of his subjects.

The first attempts at the reform of Kalahari local government came in the early 1960s. In 1961 advisory African Local Councils were set up to consult with the District Commissioner, but these ill-conceived and impotent bodies were taken seriously by nobody. A more successful move was the establishment of the Ghanzi School Committee in 1964. It had begun to make itself felt under the leadership of a local Democratic Party leader when it was scrapped and replaced by a new body. These were unimportant harbingers of more radical developments. National Independence was at hand, and even the Kalahari Crown Lands were exposed to winds of change.

III

The Bechuanaland Democratic Party (BDP)[1] arrived in the Kalahari in 1962–3, shortly after its foundation. It moved from the line of rail to Matseng and then into Ghanzi District. The Ghanzi branches were organised during a rapid tour undertaken by the Matseng leader and two influential men from Nojane. Meetings were held in each of the villages, and village committees elected.

This marked the emergence of the 'new men' in District affairs and the extension of their influence at the village level. They were younger men than the leading village elders, generally more literate than their peers, and with longer experience of paid labour, often as skilled workers or clerks. Some had been court-scribes or cattle-guards (low-level civil-service positions in the villages). A few had started entrepreneurial ventures. (Schoolteachers did not enter politics in the Kalahari—they were seldom local men.) Several of them were members

---

[1] Now the governing Botswana Democratic Party. It is often referred to by its nickname, *Domkrag* (automobile jack). I shall talk of the BDP, the Democratic Party or simply the 'Party'.

of junior branches of a ruling house in a village, and they had often been men of influence in village councils.

Harry Jankie of Nojane, who became unpaid District organiser of the Party in Ghanzi District, was the outstanding representative of the new leadership there. He had been a labour migrant in South Africa, an assistant in a white-owned store in the Kalahari, and a cattle-guard. He was married to a schoolmistress and was fluent in English. Although he came from a minority Tswana group in Nojane, he was a man of some inherited wealth, and enjoyed great prestige and influence in his village and throughout the District. As a cattle-guard he had achieved a reputation for fairness and consideration.

In recent years he had invested part of his capital in a truck, with which he operated a small transport business. This took him frequently to the comparatively developed south-east of the country, where he came into contact with the leaders of the newly-formed BDP. He was involved from the first in the Party's activities in the Kalahari, and in the latter part of 1963 and in 1964 he regularly toured the villages in Ghanzi District, holding meetings at which he passed on information about developments in the country and within the Party, and dealing with the questions of the villagers.

The immediate success of the BDP in the Kalahari was based largely on the qualifications of its leader, Seretse Khama, and its image of the country's future. Khama was a famous name, and Seretse's personal history had made him a hero to Africans throughout the country. Moreover, he personified all the traditional and modern attributes of leadership respected by the Kalahari people. He was the rightful heir to the most powerful chieftancy in the country, and he had been educated in universities in South Africa and Britain.

The appeal of BDP policy, while oversimplified by the villagers, was strong. The court-scribe of Kuli, who was converted early while on a visit to Lobatsi, put it like this:

In Lobatsi I went to the BPP [the opposition to the BDP] I heard them say, Let us chase the Europeans out at once. Then I went to the *Domkrag* [BDP], who said, Don't chase them out immediately—they have much to teach us. They have protected us for a long time, let us not take Independence with fighting. Let us get the Whites to teach us the atom bomb, how to make materials, and so on, and send our children overseas to study these things. Then I saw that the BDP stood for peace, and I joined them.[1]

[1] This view, which fairly epitomises the main trend of village thinking before the elections, was not too great a distortion of the party platform. See, for example, the BDP's 'Objects and Principles', and the pre-Independence issues of the Party paper, *Therisanyo*.

At the same time the BDP took a strong stand against racial discrimination, and even urged the Bantu peoples in the Kalahari to adopt a more liberal attitude to the Bushmen.

The main opposition to the BDP, Mr Matante's Bechuanaland Peoples' Party [BPP], never gained a foothold in the Kalahari in the pre-Independence period. They lacked the financial resources of the BDP as well as the organisational strength, and neither their leader nor their policy had much attraction to the people in the Kalahari. In contrast to Seretse Khama, Matante was seen as a suspicious figure. He was, one villager remarked, 'The son of a prostitute in Francistown' [i.e. of obscure origins], and was 'surrounded by people from other countries, like Johannesburg'. And while Matante's followers in Francistown periodically got into well-publicised difficulties with the police, Government was clearly well-disposed to the BDP. The BPP began to make some headway in western Botswana only after Independence, when the Hukuntsi sub-chief and some of his headmen became disaffected with the BDP Government; but they never penetrated Ghanzi District.

At the regular BDP meetings (usually addressed by Jankie in Ghanzi District), the Party's message was constantly repeated, the Party paper, *Therisanyo*, was distributed, and extracts were read aloud, and the villagers were encouraged to state their views. A major grievance of the villagers was the hunting restrictions enforced by Government. They also complained about the behaviour of Afrikaans farmers and traders, and pressed for the development of the schools, the water resources, etc. These were the issues which were normally brought to the District Commissioner's attention when he visited the villages, but now Jankie undertook to carry the message himself to the District capital, indicating that with Seretse Khama behind him the District authorities would have to pay attention. However, for some time the District Administration did not regard him as a serious or legitimate spokesman for the villagers.

IV

In April 1964 the details of a new constitution for Bechuanaland were settled, and within a year the territory was granted internal self-government as a prelude to full political independence. The new constitution provided for both a 'House of Chiefs' and an elective 'Legislative Assembly'. Since the people of Ghanzi District did not have a paramount chief of any kind, they were asked to choose one of their headmen to represent them as 'sub-chief' in the projected upper house.[1] At the same time the BDP instructed its branches to select candidates for the constituencies. (Both Ghanzi and Kgalagadi Districts were declared constituencies.) These developments initiated a brief and novel phase of popular politics in the Kalahari Districts.

In November 1964 delegates selected by the village councils in Ghanzi District assembled near the Mamono camp (a central and neutral place) to choose a candidate for the constituency. There were two contenders for the nomination, Jankie and an Ngologa man from Kalkfontein named Babish. Babish had been a railway's policeman in South West Africa and he now owned a small store in Kalkfontein. He had a genealogical claim to the Kalkfontein headmanship, belonging to a recently excluded line, and he had been influential in village affairs. He spoke good English and Afrikaans.

The Kalkfontein representatives tried to persuade their fellow-Ngologa from Kuli village to support Babish, on the grounds that the country had traditionally 'belonged to the Ngologa'. The Kuli people preferred Jankie, however, who though a Tswana came from a neighbouring village and was well-known to them and highly respected. The other delegates—Tswana and Herero from Karakobis and Makunda—supported Jankie. The Kuli delegates were confirmed in their temporary deviation from Ngologa solidarity by Jankie's assurance that the forthcoming appointment of a sub-chief for the District would certainly go to one of the Ngologa headmen.

The Kalkfontein delegates held firm for Babish, arguing that in the Kalkfontein council the headman and tribe had categorically refused to consider the nomination of a Tswana man. A compromise was finally agreed upon. The names of Jankie and Babish would both be submitted to Party headquarters, and the Party leaders would be left to choose between them.

The Party leaders, however, asked the Ghanzi people to reconsider the issue. In the following month a meeting was held at Kalkfontein. At first the dominant local Ngologa were extremely aggressive. They attacked Tswana District officials who were present in speeches and generally showed an unconciliatory attitude towards the prospect of a Tswana representative. On the second day of the meeting the

[1] Government did not plan to give the new 'sub-chief' authority over other headmen in the District, as had been done in the case of Northern Kgalagadi District. It was no longer policy to increase the powers of 'traditional authorities', and in any case, in Government's view, none of the Ghanzi headmen had the qualities necessary to make a good 'paramount'.

Herero headman of Makunda, who was neutral as between the Ngologa
and Tswana, proposed a compromise. Jankie should be nominated, but
Babish should be his deputy and assistant. Someone pointed out that
the two men would not be allowed to enter the Legislative Assembly
together. Jankie replied that if he fell ill Babish could deputise for him,
and he added that he would be pleased to be accompanied by a Ngologa
man who could advise and criticise him.

When the Party headquarters heard of these developments they
feared that the nomination of either Jankie or Babish might provoke
the followers of the rival candidate to mount a maverick campaign.
Accordingly they nominated an outsider, a Tswana man from the east
of the country, who had never even visited the District. This might
have been risky, but in the event no opposition was organised and he
was returned unopposed at the election. (The BDP also captured
Kgalagadi District without a fight, and won an overwhelming
majority of seats in the new Legislative Assembly.)[1]

Despite the failure of Jankie's manoeuvre, the deal he had proposed
went through and the Ngologa headman of Kalkfontein became sub-
chief of Ghanzi District with a seat in the House of Chiefs. This was in
any case a fairly predictable choice. Kalkfontein is the largest and oldest
village in the District, and the ruling Thyaga sub-clan is the senior of
the Ngologa groups in the District.

The contrast between the values reflected in the selection of a sub-
chief and the dispute over the nomination of a parliamentary candidate
is interesting. Debates in the villages revealed early that people wanted
a 'new man', educated and modern in outlook, to represent them in
the Legislative Assembly. As one villager remarked, 'someone clever
must be chosen, for the Boers are really against us'. (The candidate
had to be English-speaking in any case, or else he could not participate
in Assembly debates.) The sub-chief, on the contrary, was chosen from
among the headmen, and on the basis of more 'traditional' criteria.
This was the intention of Government, but villagers also argued that
it was a good thing because while the member of the Legislative
Assembly could be voted out of office, the sub-chief was appointed
for life.

Further, 'tribal' loyalties were less significant in the choice of a
candidate for the Legislative Assembly than in the choice of a sub-chief.
The fact that the Kuli delegates supported Jankie reflects this. (It is true
that the appeal of the Kalkgontein delegates was couched in 'tribal'

[1] In the 1969 elections, Jankie was the BDP candidate and was returned unopposed.

terms, but they were engaged in special pleading for one of their fellow-citizens.)

What these events demonstrated was the emergence of the 'new men' of the District in a new sphere of political action, resting their claims for support on the novel basis that they were modern men who were in touch with national developments and who could effectively make the voices of the villagers heard in the places of power. But even these new men recognised that the 'traditional' leaders had their own legitimate sphere of political activity, which at this stage they did not challenge in any way.

The last stage of this flurry of pan-village political activity came with the election of District Councillors shortly before Botswana's independence in 1966. Each Kalahari village returned one District Councillor. These elections, however, were controlled by the Democratic Party. In Ghanzi, the new Member of the Legislative Assembly toured the District with Jankie and held meetings in each village at which the villagers agreed on their candidates. The Coloured and European areas were similarly organised. The BDP was so confident of its control of the villagers, that it advised the new Councillors to elect a European chairman of the Council—in the interests of a broad national multiracial strategy. (Both Jankie and his old rival Babish were nominated for the post of vice-chairman, but on lots being drawn, Jankie was appointed.)

The new District Councils in the Kalahari are very important, but administratively rather than politically. They have strengthened the District Administration and made it more flexible, but they have not fundamentally politicised it. The Councils in the Kalahari are not split internally into factions—or at least, not yet—and they are unlikely to challenge the District Commissioner's control of District affairs in the near future. The key achievement of the African District Councillors has been to draw the village and the District Administration a little closer together. They have a crucial position in the communication network, which they have greatly improved.

This brief period of District level African politics has had two main legacies: the improvement of communication between village and District headquarters, and the institutionalisation of the political role of the 'new men'. I have been examining these developments mainly at the District level, but they have had repercussions in the villages as well. Today the District Councillor shares with the headman the leadership of the village community, and within weeks of his election he was already having a major impact on the way in which the villagers managed their communal affairs.

To sum up, a series of changes initiated at the top have centralised and developed local government over the past generation. Recent attempts to broaden participation in decision-making at the District level have succeeded in part. Communication between the District Administration and the village has improved, and the 'new men' of the District have been brought into the councils of the District Commissioner and confirmed as political leaders at the village level. However, the captains and the kings have not departed.

4

THE VILLAGE HEADMAN

I

Fortes once remarked that 'among the Ashanti a lineage may select the proper elder to administer its internal affairs and represent it in traditional relationships, and some Western-trained young man to represent it in his relations with the Colonial Government'.[1] This observation is pertinent to the Kalahari situation. Most of the village headmen and their counsellors are illiterate and do not speak English, and few have had the experience, common among younger men, of some schooling, or of migrant labour in neighbouring countries. Yet the villagers are constantly involved with the 'modern' wider world—selling livestock, skins and labour; buying food, clothes and even luxuries; educating their children; investing in boreholes; dealing with the District or State bureaucracy; joining political parties, and so on.

Some of these problems can be solved fairly easily with the help of the younger generation. Letters can be dictated to or deciphered by a schoolteacher or even a schoolchild, and one's son may be able to handle cattle-receipts. Some communal action is possible along similar lines. For example, when an Afrikaner cattle-buyer came to Kuli village, the villagers bargained through one of the headman's sons while another, who had worked for many years in South West Africa, interpreted. A grandson of the headman then checked the payments.

Government has also recognised the difficulties, and court-scribes have been appointed in each village to assist the headman. The court-scribe is often a close kinsman of the headman, but he is always literate and typically younger than the average headman, though not always very strong in English. He is paid the same salary as the headman by Government. His duties include recording the judgments of the village court, passing on instructions from the District Commissioner and police, and assisting in minor administrative jobs—for example, he helps the District tax-collector and the cattle-guard. He is an important link in the communication chain between the village and the District authorities.

[1] Quoted by Gluckman, 1963: 41–2.

The court-scribe normally obeys instructions from the headman and is rarely a threat to his authority, although his civil service status and salary does allow him a certain freedom of action. For example, a court-scribe may report to the District Commissioner that some villagers have failed to pay their fines, when the headman would prefer to deal with the matter internally, in order to avoid alienating the defaulters.

Few court-scribes, however, are among the local adventurers in modernisation, the 'new men' who command the respect of the villagers as men-of-the-world and people who take daring economic initiatives, buying lorries or setting up stores. These are men who left the Kalahari for long periods in South Africa or South West Africa, returned with capital which they invested in new ways, and who began to deal with the outside world on new terms. In the early 1960s they organised some communal cattle-drives to the Lobatsi abbatoir, so that the villagers would not have to sell at low prices to local buyers. As I have shown, they brought the Democratic Party to the Kalahari, and with the election of District Councillors from the villages in 1966 their political role was institutionalised. They were now the main mediators between the District authorities and the villagers. This immediately gave them positions of greatly enhanced authority within the villages.

In most villages the District Councillor now shares the leadership with the headman. In Nojane a man addressed his fellow-citizens as members of 'the village council of Headman A and "Chairman" Mr B (the District Councillor)'. This neatly sums up the situation. The District Councillors lead the village council when it discusses matters on which authoritative decisions are taken in the District Council or the Party, and more generally when a novel issue involves close dealings with outside agencies. When issues of this kind are being discussed, he may actually chair the council session. He is also better placed than the headman to push the villagers into making decisions, because he is better informed and has an external power base in the District Council and Party which overshadows the headman's official link with the District Commissioner. He is, moreover, normally detached from the kin-based village factions.

Some District Councillors head movements aimed at introducing 'progressive' measures in the village—e.g. the establishment of marketing and distributive cooperatives, bans on trapping near the village, etc. At least two Kalahari District Councillors have built up pressure groups of like-minded men to help them pass such measures through the village council. If their policies fail they have the option of transferring an issue from the village council to the District Council. For instance a solution proposed by some District Councillors in Ghanzi to the inefficient village management of Government boreholes was to set a fee for their use, assessed on the basis of an individual's stockholdings, and to administer the levy through the District Treasury.

This revolution has not stripped the headman of all authority, but rather created a channel for the management of the external—or 'modern'—affairs of the villagers. The only opposition to this development has come from the Hukuntsi sub-chief and some of his allies. I have already noted his special position, and he stands out among the Kalahari headmen on account of his education and his command of English. It seems possible that these new developments may even strengthen the headman in certain aspects of his role: after all, he remains unchallenged as the judge and the symbol of the village corporation, and the complications of coping with the new world have been largely resolved.

II

The difficulty faced by the headman and many of his subjects in coping with modern economic and political circumstances should be distinguished from another source of stress, which derives from what Gluckman has termed the 'inter-calary' nature of his role. For the past generation the headman has been at the same time the leader of his people and a servant of Government. His tribesmen expect him to represent their interests to the Administration, while the Administration tends to expect him to behave like a Government servant, representing the interests of the Administration in his village.[1] This dual constraint is fundamental in shaping the headman's role. It is in these terms that one must examine recruitment to office and its legitimation, the checks on the headman's power, and the definition of his duties and perquisites.

Increasingly in the post-war years the District Commissioners controlled the headmen. In the late 1940s, they decided which headmen in the Kalahari should be granted recognition and a salary. For example, in 1947, the Ghanzi District Commissioner reported to the Resident

---

[1] See Gluckman, Mitchell and Barnes, 1949, reprinted as Chapter 5 of Gluckman, 1963. Gluckman reviews the development of his thinking on this issue and discusses relevant literature in Gluckman, 1963: 41–4.

Commissioner (after making a tour of his District to explain the new
Native Administration Proclamation):

Ramoŝwane (Kgalagari) 16 miles north of Headman Keakopa (Barolong)[1]
Nojane said he considered he should be a Native Authority and was not
pleased to be merely a member of the Keakopa Native Authority Council.
He has 32 tax payers and Keakopa 104. I told him I would bring the matter
to your notice. He did not impress me as being an authoritative person,
indeed his first remark to me, at his kraal, was that his people did not show
him sufficient respect and that he had difficulty in keeping some of them in
order.

Accordingly he advised against the recognition of Ramoŝwane, and
the Resident Commissioner concurred. But the rapid turnover of
District Commissioners, each with considerable individual authority,
did not make for continuity or consistency. In 1950 a new District
Commissioner reported:

Although Headman Keakopa has a bigger following than Ramoŝwane, he is
a comparative newcomer to these parts . . . Ramoŝwane, a Mongologa, is
recognised by all including Keakopa as a headman of at least equal rank to
Keakopa . . . He is a person of stature in the district both physically and in
personality, and has been recognised by Government at least to the extent
of being paid Tax Commission every year. Why he has never been gazetted
as a Native Authority under section 12 and sub-section (1) of section 13 of
Proclamation No. 32 of 1943, I cannot say.[2]

And so Ramoŝwane was gazetted a subordinate Native Authority and
granted a small salary.

The Kalahari people recognise that Botswana's independence has
brought African participation at the top, and that this implies greater
accessibility to the people who wield power, but they accept also the
fact of the continued dominance of the District Commissioner at the
local level. They have always tended to personify Government
(*gorumente*). In colonial days they saw it as a hierarchy of individuals,
headed by the Queen, with the Resident Commissioner below her and
the District Commissioner as the local representative. Today—one
man remarked in the village council—things are much the same. The
people have been cheated. Seretse has just sent his in-laws (i.e. the

---

[1] The District Commissioner was wrong. Headman Keakopa is in fact a Tlharo, and his
village is only about eleven miles from Ramoŝwane's.

[2] Both these quotations come from reports in the Ghanzi District office. The second
official, Mr Midgely, was unusually well-informed, and he is still remembered by the
villagers as an outstanding District Commissioner.

British) to rule the people.[1] But the fact of overrule remains un-questioned and unchallenged.

In these circumstances one can see why headmen should often justify their positions by reference to European recognition. For example, Headman Ramoŝwane of Kuli, facing criticism from his subjects and the threat of complaints to the District Commissioner, told his village council:

I collected much money for England. I am well known by the Resident Commissioner, by King George VI and ... and ... that woman [after prompting:] Elizabeth. Now I am old and people treat me lightly. They want to take away my chair of ruling. But I shall step down only for Matlopelwe my son, and I shall not be driven out by fear.

And on another occasion, asserting Ngologa claims to primacy in the District in his village council, he said: 'The Europeans gave a gun to old Leswape [his father]. They asked who was headman, and Leswape identified himself ... Long ago this country was for the Ngologa.' The villagers accept the situation, and I often heard the remark (not necessarily critical): 'The headman is just the District Commissioner.'

Nevertheless both Government and, even more, the villagers, demand traditional qualifications for headmanship as well. The District Commissioners recognised only men who had a genealogical title to the headmanship. The villagers themselves believe that the headman's right to rule derives basically from his position, fixed by descent, within the founding sub-clan. The sub-clan which arrived first at a suitable pan sank a well and marked prominent trees in the neighbourhood to signify their claim to a village. The genealogically senior man in the sub-clan normally became headman, although the headmanship might be kept open if more senior members of the group were expected to join the settlement. The Ngologa talk of a sub-clan as a corporate group, and they say that a village is owned by the sub-clan which first staked a claim to it. As it is sometimes expressed, they rule *kga širiba*, by virtue of the well. The headman's authority is thus represented as a consequence of his senior genealogical position within the founding sub-clan.

Neither the District authorities nor the villagers have ever been inflexible, however. The ideal picture has always been liable to altera-tion in the interests of having a competent and just headman. This principle of fitness to rule may in extreme cases be dominant. Leswape I

[1] It will be remembered that Sir Seretse is married to an Englishwoman, the former Miss Ruth Williams.

provides an extraordinary example. He became headman of Lehututu despite the fact that he was not even from the incumbent's sub-clan. It appears that the incumbent was an incompetent headman, and without respect for the law. Leswape I, who was one of his counsellors, was already carrying the administration of the village when he took over the headmanship with the general support of the citizens. His descendants continue to rule Lehututu. The family of the ousted headman remained in the village, and apparently accept the justice of the situation.

More commonly, however, alternative candidates are found within the ruling family, and conflicting claims sometimes allow room for manoeuvre. The Kgalagadi District Commissioner, confronted with several claimants for the Hukuntsi headmanship after the Second World War, chose one mainly because he was an exserviceman with a good record. The emphasis on fitness to rule also underlies the common practice of retiring headmen when they become too old and inactive to rule efficiently.

The Ngologa also assert that a man is a rightful ruler only if he respects the *molao*. *Molao* is a multi-referential term with many of the connotations of the English word 'law'. It covers social and natural regularities, bodies of rules, customs, instructions from senior to juniors, laws of the type the court enforces, and in its broadest political sense, the 'constitution'.[1] When a headman acts in a manner proper to his role he 'is' the law. If he is held to be acting wrongly, people say he is spoiling (*šinya*) the law. The law rules, *molao ke pusho*, and the headman is identified with the law only so long as he rules constitutionally.

The interplay of the various factors which go to make a headman are dramatised by succession disputes. The history of the Kalkfontein headmanship—the oldest in Ghanzi District—exemplifies the interplay of traditional claims, personal qualities, political strategy and the actions of the District Commissioner.

The Kalkfontein succession disputes

Kalkfontein was founded in the first decade of the twentieth century by migrating pastoralists led by a man named Sikeleri. Sikeleri was herding

---

[1] *Molao* is a central concept in all Sotho-speaking areas, and it has merited the attention of several anthropologists. See Schapera, 1955: 35–6, and especially Gluckman, 1955: 164 ff. (Any ruler may also be called *molauri*, but this term is normally reserved for the District Commissioner.)

some cattle belonging to his senior agnate, Kolwane, and he informed the responsible Government officer that his 'older brother' Kolwane would in due course come and assume the headmanship. Before this plan could be carried out, a more senior group of the same (Thayga) clan settled in the village under the leadership of Babish. However, Babish died prematurely in a battle against the Hottentots, and his son Tsaawe, then a young man, conceded the headmanship to Kolwane.

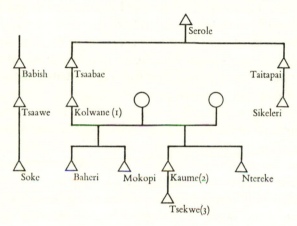

Fig. 5. The headmen of Kalkfontein.

When Kolwane retired as an old man in the late 1920s, Babish's line claimed the headmanship, but a younger son of Kolwane, Kaume, succeeded. According to possibly biased informants, he was preferred to Kolwane's two older sons because he was very able while they were very stupid.

Kaume went blind in his old age and gradually dropped out of active political life. His younger brother Ntereke managed the affairs of the village while the succession was being settled. The strongest claimant was Kaume's first son, Tšekwe. Although Tšekwe was the child of a not entirely respectable first love, his mother's liason with Kaume had been legitimised by the payment of *bogari* (bridewealth) by Kolwane himself. Tšekwe was by no means Kaume's favourite son, and he had spent many years of his life with his mother's people in Ngamiland. Nevertheless, Ntereke supported Tšekwe. The main alternative was Babish's grandson Soke, who, some people assert today, enjoyed at least tacit support from Kaume.

The main act of the drama may usefully be considered from two points of view: as it appeared to the shrewd District Commissioner,

Midgely, and as it is recalled by politically active villagers. Midgely records that he visited Kaume at his sick-bed in November 1950. Kaume told him that he was worried about a split in his tribe and wanted Tšekwe to succeed. On the following day a meeting of the villagers was held. In response to the request of the villagers, the other headmen in the District attended. To Midgely's understandable surprise a message was brought from Kaume by Ntereke and another senior counsellor that 'I have no child or uncle to name'. The District Commissioner despatched another delegation to the sick-bed, which returned with a new statement from Kaume. According to the delegates, Kaume now said, 'I had my brother Ntereke in mind as he has always been my helper; but now, as there is dissension in the tribe, my son Tšekwe is the man I name to be my successor'.[1]

The 'inside story' is somewhat different. When the succession dispute was coming to a head, Ntereke sent Tšekwe to Ghanzi. A meeting was held in the village to consider the succession, but Ntereke successfully argued that the matter could not be discussed in Tšekwe's absence. Tšekwe then returned with Midgely. Midgely sent Ntereke to ask Kaume who should succeed him, and he came back with Tšekwe's name. There is no doubt that using Midgely, Ntereke was able to steamroller the opposition. Even now some people assert that Ntereke and Tšekwe bought Midgely.

It is extremely difficult to work out today what the precise structure of the various factions was, but the main outline of the political manoeuvres is fairly clear. The point I wish to stress is that while Tšekwe obviously had the backing of powerful forces within the village, a critical element in ensuring his succession was Ntereke's skill in manipulating the District Commissioner into supporting him.

Midgely was also satisfied that Tšekwe was the rightful claimant who could command widespread support, and that he would make an adequate Government representative. The villagers on their side had ensured that whoever succeeded would be a legitimate headman in the traditional sense. This was done by inviting the other headmen in the District to attend the meeting. These outsiders, who are not themselves eligible for the succession, represent the *molao*, and they instruct the new headman and the tribe in their new duties.[2] Immediately Kaume's

[1] Midgely's reports are in the Ghanzi District office.
[2] Commenting on parallel procedures in West Africa, Fortes writes, 'It is a cardinal rule that these electors must not themselves be eligible for the succession, nor may those who can succeed to the ruler's office hold an elector's office. The electors are, in effect, the agents of the tribe and custodians of the body of law and custom' (1962: 71).

final choice had been accepted, Headman Ramoŝwane of Kuli told the assembly, 'It is right that Kaume's eldest son should take his place, particularly as his father has confirmed it'. He added that the other contenders should be made counsellors of the new headman, and concluded, 'the tribe must cooperate, not split up and continue with petty jealousies'.

Midgely describes how once his succession had been assured Tsekwe said, 'The headman and District Commissioner arranged for my death. The people say of me, "can such a bad man stay with people?" I ask for Ntereke to assist me in this difficult job.'[1] The meeting closed at last with a prayer led by a local evangelist who asked that God should give Tsekwe wisdom, like Solomon.

Succession disputes are resolved by an interplay of factional manoeuvres and the power of outside authorities; and they occur within a framework of values which derive from the indigenous political system and from the contemporary local government structure. A recent case in Kang indicates that a new element has now been introduced, at least in Northern Kgalagadi District. Rivals for headmanship align themselves with different political parties, and their factions use the idiom of party-political conflict. In any case, succession to the headmanship is normally the subject of some dispute, and the crisis tends to crystallise village factions for the next generation.

III

My argument is that the headman's role is conditioned by two sets of social forces, one intra-village the other external; one 'traditional' the other 'bureaucratic'. I have tried to show how both are involved in the struggle for succession and in the legitimation of the headmanship. Each is associated also with a particular set of rights, duties and perquisites. These do not always overlap, and sometimes conflict.

The advent of British overrule and the social changes which have increasingly affected the Kalahari over the past thirty years have had a considerable impact on the powers and duties of the headman. Government has limited his judicial competence, while placing new sanctions at his disposal and imposing new duties on him, including the collection of taxes, the raising of educational levies and so forth.

[1] Tsekwe's comment that the headman and District Commissioner had 'arranged for his death' should be compared with similar reactions among the Fort Jameson Ngoni, described in Barnes's contribution to Gluckman, Mitchell and Barnes, 1949.

The appointment of court-scribes and the election of District Council-lors made inroads on his former position as sole political leader. More diffuse forces of change have resulted in the disappearance of his rain-making magic and brought about the decline of the age-regiments, on which he formerly depended for many purposes. Finally, he must now cope with new demands from his people.

As I have already said, the specific tasks imposed on the headman by Government have dwindled with the increasing specialisation of administration. Court-scribes, tax-collectors and now District Council-lors have relieved him of the burden of a number of duties which were imposed upon him when the District Administration was first estab-lished. The District Councillor also deals with a number of demands from the people with which the headman had inadequately struggled to cope.

From the point of view of Government, the headman is now seen as adequate if he maintains peace in the village. There must not be too many complaints and appeals to the District Commissioner. The headman is always conscious that he is liable to be adjudged too old to be modern, and so must be on his toes, but as long as he meets these minimum requirements, the District Commissioner will support him.

The duties with which the modern headman is left derive from his traditional prerogative as 'owner' of the village and the village council. He is chairman of the council and its principal administrative agent; he can grant or withhold citizenship from prospective im-migrants, and forbid or permit foreigners to sink wells or operate cattle-posts in his territory; he must entertain strangers, and is respon-sible for their safety; he must organise his people for defence against enemies or predatory beasts; and he must organise collective labour for communal projects. These duties must be performed to the satisfaction of his subjects and without upsetting the District authorities, and so while they are 'traditional' duties the headman's execution of them is judged in part from a 'bureaucratic' standpoint.

Perhaps the most important on-going functions of the headman are those associated with his position as chairman and executive of the village council, the decision-making body on a wide range of political and judicial issues. Here, too, many of the burgeoning problems of modern political and economic life have been taken over by the District Councillor, who now chairs the council when issues of this type are being discussed. The headman remains with control of the day-to-day administrative business and with supreme judicial authority, an aspect of the headman's role always stressed by villagers. He is also responsible for arranging council-sessions and seeing to it that the decisions are implemented. This range of responsibility incapsulates much of the village political system, as will be evident in later chapters.

The other main duties of the headman centre on the preservation and development of the village estate. Water is the crucial valuable, and the headman must ensure that his people have an adequate supply for themselves and their livestock. Some headmen have used personal resources to help subsidise the sinking of boreholes. When the rains fail the headman should see to it that evangelists are brought in to pray for rain, or that Bushmen are paid to do rain-dances. If there is pressure on the water resources of the village, he should check immigration. In drought years particularly, African pastoralists from dry and over-grazed areas try to move into more favoured villages, or at least to get watering rights in them. Kuli is periodically under pressure in this respect. Headmen are usually ready to help in such cases, but they cannot permit the scarce water-resources under their control to be unduly exploited by outsiders. Prospective immigrants who have close kin in the village will usually be granted citizenship, and there is a tendency for Ngologa headmen to favour Ngologa immigrants.

The headman should also organise action against predators which threaten the village herds. Until quite recently a communal hunt would have been the answer,[1] but with the diffusion of firearms the headman is more likely now to call on expert hunters in his own or a neighbouring village.

Human enemies are no longer the threat they were in the anarchic nineteenth century, when the people of the Kalahari were involved in endless minor engagements, or in the early years of the twentieth century, when armed Hottentot bands, escaping from German West Africa, marauded Kgalagari groups. Defence may, however, still be a real responsibility in villages near the South West African border, which are regularly infiltrated by South West African police in pursuit of cattle-thieves, runaway Bushmen labourers and political refugees. I was present in Kuli on one occasion when a report was brought to the headman that two or three armed South West African police were searching the outskirts of his village, presumably in pursuit of a Bushman stock-thief. The headman immediately armed three young men with his own rifles, mounted them on his horses, and sent them

[1] For an eye-witness account of a communal Kgalagari lion-hunt, see Schapera, 1932.

after the infiltrators. The villagers chased the policemen across the border, but failed to apprehend them.

The headman's duty to care for visitors and to protect them has also involved some headmen near the border in conflicts with South West African police, for they have harboured political refugees from across the border until they could be transported to other centres in the country on their way north. All visitors should be brought to the headman on arrival in the village, and unless they have kin living there he will see to it that they are looked after.

It is difficult nowadays for the headman to organise labour for collective enterprises. Since the growth of the primary schools in the 1940s, no new age-regiments have been formed. In any case most of the young men who in the past would have been in the forefront of such work are away on migrant labour. If they are in the village they generally refuse to work without monetary rewards. In Kuli tasks requiring collective labour, such as the maintenance of the school and of the teachers' quarters are often not carried out at all, or are performed by a few old men of the headman's own regiment as best they can. In other villages various techniques are being used to tackle this problem. The Hukuntsi sub-chief controls a small treasury, and he pays wages to labourers on some communal projects. In Kalkfontein the matter has been taken out of the headman's hands. The village branch of the BDP raises cash levies and then pays a few skilled labourers to perform the necessary work. Finally, in the early 1960s, Government organised famine-relief programmes which were later taken over by the District Councillors and used to support villagers working on communal projects.

IV

The headman's sources of power and the remedies of the people have also been altered by overrule. Ngologa headmen have never been very powerful, dependent always on majority backing and aiming at consensus. Now the police are at call, and they and the District Commissioner are generally ready to bolster his authority. The headman may threaten to play these cards, and even win a trick or two in this way, but unless the support he gets from these outside authorities is constant, he is bluffing. Even the Hukuntsi sub-chief, who gambled on this support in the most favourable of conditions, nearly lost his position as a result of unrest among his people. Conversely, District Commissioners may remove headmen, and the fact that his people can complain about him to the District Commissioner is a check on the headman's use of power.

The main bar to autocracy, however, remains the dependence of the headman on his people. The District authorities—except to some degree at Matšeng—have not been close enough or sufficiently predictable to present the headman with an effective alternative source of power. His subjects retain their most potent defensive weapon, passive non-cooperation. No headman can force his people to cooperate in running the day-to-day affairs of the village, or participate in what Government regards as voluntary activities, or even ensure that the influential villagers attend at the council-place. And without their participation, the headman can do very little.

Another traditional defence against an autocratic headman was secession, and even the threat of succession could be a major check on a headman's abuse of power. Today secession is rare, for a variety of reasons. The water-sources of the Kalahari are fairly well-occupied, and Government discourages large-scale migrations which might lead to jurisdictional disputes and other difficulties. Further, access to bore-holes, roads and schools is now a major consideration—in fact a number of smaller and more isolated settlements have been abandoned. On the other hand, as a number of informants pointed out to me, the benefits of secession are minimal nowadays since 'now the *molao* ("law") is the same everywhere'. Switching one's allegiance from one headman to another does not bring alleviation of taxation or freedom from other unpopular impositions of the State. Nevertheless, secession is still used as a last resort—the Hukuntsi sub-chief has lost a number of subjects in this way. A more popular compromise is to form a hamlet at some distance from the headman's settlement, establishing a degree of *de facto* independence.

v

The rewards of office have also been altered by the new situation of the headman within a local government hierarchy, and he has lost the strategic economic position he once commanded within the community. In living memory the headman was given portions of cattle which were slaughtered, or game which was hunted in his territory, and also the skins of certain animals and other forms of tribute. All these kinds of tribute were known as *sehuba* (breast), since this was the portion of a carcass set aside for the headman. Nowadays tribute is no longer rendered in the old style. People feel that modern taxes have taken its place. To pay tax to a headman is a recognition of his sovereignty over one, as was the payment of tribute. The difference is that taxes do not enrich the headman, nor can they be redistributed among his subjects. They are paid into the District Treasury, as are the fines levied in the headman's court. Other old sources of wealth have also been cut off—the impounding of stray stock (*matimela*), for example, and cattle-raiding.

There are compensations. The headman's power of patronage has increased. He has a good deal of influence over the allocation of the new, paid offices which Government has established in the village. In most villages there is a borehole 'pumper', a court-scribe and a cattle-guard. Even if local or external pressures prevent the headman securing such a position for a member of his family-group or a loyal supporter, the man who gets the job is involved in the 'government' of the village. He is therefore to some degree under the headman's control, and he is inhibited in the use of the strategy of non-cooperation.

The headman is also paid a salary. It has recently been increased to R80 (about £47 p.a.), but although this is not negligible it does not compare favourably with other opportunities to make cash. The headmen are generally among the richest villagers, and in Kuli and Lehututu they are far and away the wealthiest. But some are out-stripped by enterprising subjects who take the modern ways to wealth, such as trading or transport-riding, or even migrant labour.

All this raises a problem for those who believe that people seek office mainly with an eye to the economic rewards, direct or indirect. Many rich men are headmen, but so are a few men who are only moderately well-off by village standards, and the headmanship does not make a man rich. One may evade the issue by arguing with Leach that it is 'necessary and justifiable to assume that a conscious or un-conscious wish to gain power is a very general motive in human affairs',[1] and leave it at that, but such an argument hardly advances our understanding. I can only attempt to mitigate the astonishment of cynics by pointing out that there are few attractive economic alterna-tives for uneducated men, and that the position is a useful extra to the accumulation and sale of cattle.

The present economic position of the headman has several implica-tions. He is no longer a distributor of largesse, and this has affected his

[1] Leach, 1954: 10. Nonetheless 'as a general rule' Leach holds 'that the social anthro-pologist is never justified in interpreting action as unambiguously directed towards any one particular end' (*ibid.*).

hold on his subjects. On the other hand, he has little economic incentive to take political risks on behalf of Government. Taken alone, his modern economic status does not make him dependent either on his people or on Government, and economic developments have in some ways lessened the dependence of his followers on him.

VI

To return to Gluckman's argument, the headman's 'intercalary' situation is evident, whichever aspect of his role one examines. Traditional values and modern demands, the dependence on his people and the power of the District Commissioner, combine to mould his office. Yet it is not true, at least for Kalahari headmen, that 'The difficulties of the headman's position are enormously aggravated in the modern political system'.[1] Many modern issues beyond his control are now looked after by other political figures, and the District authorities cannot exert constant pressures on him. The District Commissioner, limited by shortage of staff and poor communications, is forced to recognise that the headman is dependent on his people, and in general the District Commissioner will accept this and support him. If anything, the present balance of forces favours the headman. This may be deduced from the success of Ntereke and Tšekwe in Kalkfontein, but it will be illustrated in greater detail when I present material on the political process in Kuli. (There is one potential threat to the headmen in the contemporary situation. Government is likely to move against the powerful hereditary chiefs in eastern Botswana, and in the process they may withdraw support from 'traditional' authorities throughout the country. This, however, is speculation.)

Turning to the position of the headmen within the village, Gluckman is inclined once more to represent him as being, inescapably, the focus of conflicting and perhaps irreconcilable pressures. He argues that 'Internally the village has a kinship constitution; it is also a political unit', and consequently, 'the main source of the ambivalence of [the headman's] position is that he is the personality in whom the domestic-kinship and the political systems intersect'.[2]

But is it very meaningful to say that 'the village has a kinship constitution'? With the possible exception of some matrilineal Central African groups, my reading of the literature suggests that even in the area with which Gluckman is dealing such a statement is far from

[1] Gluckman, 1963: 152.　　　　　[2] Gluckman, 1963: 149, 151.

illuminating.[1] Among the Ngologa the kinship idiom is applied to a variety of situations (though not exclusive of other modes of concep-tualisation), and, in the almost meaningless phrase, one could probably fit most villagers on to a single genealogy. Moreover, village factions are largely kin-based. In these marginal senses the village may be said to have a 'kinship constitution', but to concentrate on this obscures the true nature of village politics and of the headman's situation.

First, alongside the kinship model of the Ngologa people, there is a political model of a territorial village community united under the sovereignty of a headman and ruled by a *molao* which overrides the claims of kinship. The unit described in the phrase *merahe wa i go kgoši*, the headman's tribe, is defined geographically, administratively and politically. It is not necessary to be a kinsman of the headman or even of any villager to become a citizen, although it does help if one belongs to the Ngologa people, who are conceived of as a giant patrilineage.

Secondly, the serious political conflicts are not between the values or claims of the kinship-domestic and politico-jural domains of village life. Nor is it useful to focus on the problem of an individual caught between these two domains, as Gluckman represents the village headman. Village politics is concerned rather with the reconciliation of conflicting interests within a political arena. That these interests are often pressed by kin-based factions is beside the point. Once this is recognised, it is easier to appreciate the true nature of the headman's position.

Thirdly, no Ngologa headman is related by kinship to all his sub-jects. In large villages his kin may be a minority. And he cannot rule only in the interests of his kin, even if this were his aim, because he is so dependent on majority backing, as I indicated earlier. Moreover, the closest kin of the headman are normally divided, and some are always his leading opponents. This point needs some development.

The headman's kin fall into three politically significant categories. First there are his close agnates, the members of his own family-group, and the people who belonged to the family-group of his father. Secondly there are the members of his sub-clan. He may be related to any of these close agnates or fellow-clansmen by ties through women as well as by descent. Thirdly there are the members of other clans to whom he is related through women.

Kinship ideology gives his close agnates the right, or the duty, to advise him and to assist him in the exercise of his authority. But it is

---

[1] I was privileged to see a manuscript note by Southwold which forced me to recognise the difficulties involved in saying that a village is a kinship unit.

also from this group that his main opponents are recruited. The opposition of close agnates, a feature of Ngologa kinship, is exacerbated when a family-group owns the headmanship. In all Ngologa villages, the closest allies and the leading opponents of a headman include brothers, father's brothers and father's brothers' sons. Paradoxically, their close agnatic connection with the headman gives their opposition some legitimacy. They are among the 'owners of the village', and it is their duty to 'advise' the headman.

The other members of his sub-clan also have a claim to be 'owners of the village' and thus to a special voice in the government. In practice this may amount to little more than the formal recognition of a rather empty status, unless they have achieved influence on a more substantial basis. It is sometimes said that members of the ruling sub-clan are favoured in the headman's court. There is little evidence for this, and as I have said, a group within the sub-clan is certain to be in opposition to the headman. The headman and his leading agnatic opponent both recruit the cores of their factions from within this group.

Affines and matrilateral kin have no automatic claim to special political status. They may use their connections as the basis of a close alliance with the headman, but as the example of Waatotsi shows, ties through women do not necessarily result in political alliance.

In short, the headman's strongest supporters are close agnates and matrilateral kin, but his major opponents are drawn from within the same circle, and a large body of his subjects—in some villages the majority—are outside the circle of his close kin, or even the wider category of his fellow-clansmen. Since he must command general support if he is to rule, the headman must look beyond the members of his kin-based faction and be seen to be 'for the tribe'. (In the words of the widespread Sotho proverb, shared by the Ngologa, *kgoši e kgoši kga merahe*, the headman is headman with, or by, the tribe.) Indeed his ultimate source of strength is that he alone symbolises the unity of the village community and its estate. His real problem is to do enough to secure this status and the normal cooperation of his subjects while looking after his own interests and those of his faction.

5

AUTHORITIES AND FACTIONS
IN THE VILLAGE

I

The headman is in many ways the leader of the village community, but he does not control it. The governing body of the village is the headman-in-council (the *lekgota*), which comprises the adult male citizens. This body is itself dominated by an informal and fairly fluid group, the 'village authorities', which includes the office-holders, who are members of the 'village government', and also leading members of the opposition and a few influential independents. I have already discussed the roles of the headman, District Councillor and court-scribe. In the following section of this chapter I deal with the village counsellors, the remaining members of the 'government'.

II

The counsellors may be divided into three groups on the basis of recruitment—chief counsellor, sub-clan heads and 'popular' counsellors. With the partial exception of the chief counsellor, they have the same duties. All may be referred to as *banawe ba kgoši*, the headman's juniors (or younger brothers); *bathanka ba kgoši*, the headman's servants; or as *macounsellor*.[1]

The chief counsellor is normally chosen by the headman to be his right-hand man, and he is often a close agnate. In Kuli the chief counsellor is headman Ramošwane's younger brother. Occasionally, however, he is included in the village government as a compromise with the opposition or on the orders of the District Commissioner, and in such a case he may not be related to the headman. For example, following his defeat in the struggle for the Kalkfontein headmanship, Soke became Tšekwe's chief counsellor after the direct intervention of the District Commissioner.

---

[1] One might add a fourth category of counsellor—the headman's close agnates who are literally *banawe ba kgoši*, and who have a claim to be consulted by him. However, they do not normally share the duties of the counsellors in practice, and the villagers do not classify them together. I do not think that they are properly members of the 'village government'.

The traditional titles of the chief counsellor are *lenkyona la kgota*, the leader of the council; *lebôgô la kgoši*, the headman's arm; or *motsolo šetolo ša kgoši*, the bearer of the headman's chair.[1] Nowadays he is more often called the headman's *foreman* or *loudspeaker*, titles at least as appropriate. He is the headman's spokesman in meetings of the *lekgota*, and he normally deputises for him in his absence. Outside the council-place he supervises the villagers and the other counsellors, sees to it that they carry out the headman's instructions, and scrutinises their demands, perhaps bringing them afterwards before the headman.

Sub-clan heads may be counsellors, but this is not automatic. Some sub-clan heads play a major administrative role, running preparatory examinations on disputes within their sectors, arbitrating, and acting as go-betweens, linking the headman and the members of their sub-clans. Such sub-clan heads are counsellors, and the headman will often have a say in their succession. Other sub-clan heads have no administrative role, even though their sub-clans may be fairly cohesive. In Kuli, the Silebe sub-clan head is not a counsellor, but two of the 'popular' counsellors come from the Silebe camp.

I call the third and usually the largest group the 'popular' counsellors, because both they themselves and the other villagers tend to stress that they are expected to secure the interests of the citizen body. They may be imposed upon the headman by public pressure. The presence of 'popular' counsellors in the village government is sometimes described as in innovation. A number of informants told me that in recent years District Commissioners have come to insist that the headman should include some active 'young' men among his counsellors. This has been taken to mean that citizens apart from the sub-clan heads and outside the headman's circle of close agnates should be appointed. Accordingly, a few influential, if generally middle-aged, men have become counsellors. But in fact the headman's counsellors have always included men whose prominence was based on popular regard for their skill in debate and in jurisprudence—Leswape I's position in Lehututu before his accession to the headmanship was apparently of this kind. It is possible that pressure from the District authorities has increased the number and influence of such men, although at least in Hukuntsi the

[1] This title recalls the duty of a younger brother to carry his elder brother's blankets on a journey, or to bring his chair to a meeting, partly in order to prevent sorcerers from tampering with them. The headman is believed to be particularly at risk from sorcery, since he is the object of envy. However, in the normal course of events the headman's chair will be brought to the council-place by a young man or a villager of little prestige.

sub-chief has used Government backing to dismiss and even to imprison counsellors who opposed him. I would suggest that this attempt to derive the legitimacy of the popular counsellors from the District Commissioner is simply a modern myth which provides them with a solid charter.

I do not wish to make too much of the special position of the popular counsellors. Citizens like a counsellor, whoever he is, if he 'speaks up to the headman and checks him', to quote one informant. Even the chief counsellor is often not completely the headman's man, as Soke bears witness in Kalkfontein. Most counsellors would probably agree with the sub-clan head who told me that his job was 'to act with the headman: to remind him of what is wrong and what is right'.

At the same time, every counsellor sees his job as mainly administrative and his duty as at least partly to the headman and even to the District Administration. Even popular counsellors may represent their authority as deriving from the headman when it suits them to do so, as may be seen in this speech which a popular counsellor made to the Kuli *lekgota*:

If I call people to the council-place they despise me. There are four counsellors, two born in the village and two from outside [i.e. two from the headman's sub-clan and two Silebe]. Even if we speak for the headman, people do not listen to us. Consellors cannot be stronger than the headman. It is the headman who has power. If people despise the headman they will not listen to the counsellors.

As the agents of the headman the counsellors are expected to help convene the *lekgota* and to organise the execution of its decisions. During *lekgota* sessions their formal duty is to assist the headman to reach a sound and just decision. When they are inclined to stress this aspect of their role, counsellors underplay their very real representative function. One Kuli counsellor told me that 'The headman just judges; the counsellors "pray" (*rapela*) the headman, and just judge a little; the men of the council hear the counsellors and "pray" them'. As a description of the decision-making process this remark succeeds only in underlining the discrepancy between this particular pious constitutional ideal and the reality. Nevertheless, because they are involved in the village government, the counsellors may be useful mediators between the headman and his opponents.

With the exception of the chief counsellor, all the counsellors have a particular responsibility for the sector of the village in which they live. They should promulgate the decisions of the village government among their neighbours and make sure that they attend meetings of the *lekgota*. They should also mediate their disputes and sift quarrels and complaints before they reach the *lekgota*. This kind of responsibility devolves upon the sub-clan heads in particular in some villages, but in Kuli these duties are shouldered by the popular counsellors, two of whom come from the Silebe sub-clan while the other two are members of Mabote's faction, the opposition Pebana faction. Finally, they should all report regularly to the headman's compound to keep him informed on developments in their sectors, and also to hear the news and to help entertain visitors.

The counsellors are not paid by Government, nor are they officially recognised as local government officers. This distinguishes them from the other members of the village government—the headman, court-scribe and District Councillor. They frequently complain of this neglect, and many counsellors regard the job as far more trouble than it is worth. The chief counsellor of Kuli told me that the District Commissioner 'did not even know his name', and he had not 'written it in his book'. Nevertheless, both the villagers and the District authorities (although to a lesser extent) regard the counsellors as in part the servants of Government. As one informant told me, 'a counsellor is like a policeman: if he comes to you, you know he comes to give the orders of the District Commissioner or of the headman'. Indeed when an official proposal was made to appoint paid policemen within the villages, people assumed that the jobs would go to the counsellors.[1]

III

The village government includes those men with official positions of political leadership. It is not, however, an élite corporate body. First, the sources of its members' authority vary. The headman has 'traditional' authority plus Government backing. The District Councillor derives his authority largely from his position as mediator of modern governmental and economic agencies. The court-scribe is partly a civil servant, but enjoys some power because he has independent access to the District authorities and controls important communication links. The counsellors are backed by the authority of the headman (and indirectly the District Commissioner), and at the same time they have semi-formal constituencies within the village.

[1] Oddly enough, emphasising the norm that counsellors should not resort to force, the Lozi told Gluckman that they should *not* be like policemen! (Gluckman, 1965: 35.)

It follows from this that the interests of the different officials may diverge, although there is a minimal sense in which they all have a special responsibility and concern to see that authoritative decisions on public affairs are made and executed.

Further, the important decisions are not made by these officials themselves acting as a group. These decisions are reached in the *lekgota* (headman-in-council), and as I have already said, this body is dominated by a group which includes the members of the village government but extends beyond them. They share a dominant position with some close agnates of the headman—both his supporters and his leading opponents—and also a few other individual villagers who neither hold official positions nor have a special kinship claim to political status. I call this effective decision-making group the village authority, and its members the authorities.

The dominance of the authorities is evident to anyone who has observed a Ngologa *lekgota* over a period of time. This may be seen, at the most obvious level, by considering attendances at *lekgota* sessions. All the citizens[1] are expected to attend regularly, and they are usually advised at least a day in advance of the time and the rough agenda of the meeting. In practice, however, the attendance of a large number of citizens is erratic.

When I carried out a census in Kuli in 1964, I found that of fifty-eight adult Ngologa men normally resident in the village, eight were away on visits in other parts of the country, and ten were absent on migrant labour. Roughly forty men might thus be expected to be in the village at any one time, and to attend sessions of the *lekgota*. However, my records of attendances at *lekgota* meetings show that while most of the men in the village attended meetings from time to time, few men came to all or even the majority of meetings. The family-group heads (roughly half the total) attended more regularly than the balance of the citizens. They are older than the average, and so are less likely to be away from the village, and in general their opinions are regarded as weightier than those of most of the younger men. Moreover, they are responsible in the *lekgota* for the minors in their groups, and they may represent the other members. But if some family-group heads missed a few meetings, this was not usually

[1] To be a citizen, a man must be accepted as such by the headman. This is symbolised by the payment of tax to him. It is also said that only a man who has been legitimised by the main bridewealth payment of *bogari* may speak in the *lekgota*. This rule is not enforced, but it emphasises the importance for political purposes of belonging to an agnatic corporation.

commented upon. On the other hand, if one of the leading citizens—one of the authorities—was absent, the meeting might be postponed, or at least a crucial item might not be considered.

The dominance of the authorities emerges more dramatically from an analysis of the contributions made to *lekgota* debates. Analysing the Kuli *lekgota* debates which I recorded in 1964, I found that eleven citizens had made 84 per cent of all contributions to debates. In 1966–7, eleven citizens made 77 per cent of all contributions to the debates which I recorded.[1]

The same material can be presented in a different way. In Table 3 I set out the number of citizens who contributed in various degrees to debates I recorded in Kuli, in 1964 and 1966–7.

Table 3. *Contributions to debates recorded in the Kuli lekgota*

No. of contributions	1–10	10–20	20–30	30–40	40–50	50–
No. of citizens						
1964 (total = 34)	23	2	2	5	1	1
1966–7 (total = 29)	18	5	2	1	1	2

There are no grey eminences in Ngologa village politics. The men who dominate *lekgota* debates dominate the decision-making process.

IV

Both in 1964 and again in 1966–7, the Kuli village authority comprised eleven men. Table 4 provides some basic data on the authorities during both these periods.

(1) *The headman, his son and his son's son:* During both periods, headman Ramošwane, his eldest son, Matlopelwe, and Matlopelwe's eldest son, Leswape, the court-scribe, made over a quarter of all

---

[1] By a contribution to a debate I mean not only speeches but also participation in exchanges of question and answer, or challenge and response. I have more or less arbitrarily decided to count participation in such an exchange as being equivalent to a speech. Although I recorded more *lekgota* sessions on my first visit than on my second—thirty-one as opposed to ten—I recorded only 433 contributions to debates in 1964 as against 401 in 1966–7. This was because I used a tape-recorder to cover some sessions in 1966–7, while I was otherwise forced to record debates by hand as they were going on, and therefore merely summarised some passages and ignored a number of informal contributions. Studying my tape-recorded data I was able to satisfy myself, however, that my other information was not significantly biased.

Table 4. *The Kuli authorities*

1964		1966–7	
Name and status	% of contributions to *lekgota* debates	Name and status	% of contributions to *lekgota* debates

(1) The village headman, his son and son's son

Ramošwane (headman)	14	Ramošwane (headman)	6
Matlopelwe (his eldest son)	11	Matlopelwe	18
Leswape (Matlopelwe's son)	9	Leswape	3
Total	34	Total	27

(2) The District Councillor (elected 1966)

		Luther	14

(3) The village counsellors

Riphoni (chief counsellor)	8	Riphoni	3
Mokgethi (Silebe popular counsellor)★	9	Mokgethi	2
Modjathoši (Silebe popular counsellor)	8	—	—
		Morimongwe (popular counsellor—Mabote's faction)	10
		Mokgethise (popular counsellor—Mabote's faction)	9
Total	25	Total	24

(4) Other influential citizens—non office-holders

Mabote (faction leader)	7	Mabote	5
Lebiki (supporter of Mabote)	5	Lebiki	4
Waatotsi, Moloise and Masime (two independents and the Silebe elder statesman)	13	—	—
		Mosonturi (owner of a cattle-post at Kuli)	3
Total	25	Total	12
Grand total	84	Grand total	77

★ Mokgethi is a Pebana by birth but in Kuli he is associated with the Silebe sub-clan.

contributions to debates. In the interval between my visits, Matlopelwe became even more prominent in village politics. Headman Ramoŝwane is ageing. There have for some time been murmurs that he should retire. He is determined that Matlopelwe should succeed him, and he is quite consciously projecting him as his successor and deputy. When he travelled to Lehututu with me in 1967, he insisted that Matlopelwe should act for him rather than his younger brother Riphoni, the chief counsellor, who had normally deputised for him in the past.

(2) *The District Councillor:* The partial eclipse of Leswape, the court-scribe, in 1966–7 is directly due to the rise of the new District Councillor, Luther. In the struggle for the BDP nomination for the Kuli District Councillor, Leswape, and Luther were pitted against one another. Luther won, and Leswape, thrown off balance by his defeat, left the village for a while and began to drink heavily. He only slowly began to regain his position. The startling rise of the District Councillor to prominence in 1966 is a point I have touched on earlier, and to which I shall return.

(3) *The village counsellors:* During both periods the village counsellors accounted for about a quarter of all contributions to debates. Riphoni, the chief counsellor, lost ground, partly because the headman chose to rely more on the heir apparent, Matlopelwe.[1]

Of the four popular counsellors, two were in the forefront during my first visit and the other two on my second. The former are both Silebe, the latter members of Mabote's faction. This should not be taken to reflect a shift of power from the Silebe to Mabote's faction, however. The two popular counsellors of Mabote's faction were away from the village for the greater part of my first visit, having migrated temporarily after a tiff with the headman. On their return, popular pressure forced them to resume their duties, although they protested that they no longer wished to be counsellors. As I mentioned in an earlier chapter, the Silebe had moved to fields at a small distance from the village during the season of my 1966–7 visit. They were therefore less in evidence, and were less punctilious about attending sessions of the *lekgota*. This probably reflected strains within the Silebe camp rather than between the Silebe and the headman, but it explains why they were partly displaced by the returned popular counsellors of Mabote's faction.

(4) *Other influential citizens:* Only two non office-holders (apart from the headman's son) retained their influence between 1964 and 1967,

[1] In 1968 I received a letter from the Kuli court-scribe informing me of Riphoni's death.

namely Mabote and Lebiki. Mabote is a younger brother of the headman and the leader of the opposition faction within the Pebana sub-
clan. Lebiki is the son of Mabote's ally and father's younger brother,
Tsenene, and the younger brother of the popular counsellor Morimomongwe.

Waatotsi, who had been an influential independent on my first visit,
left the village to make an extended visit to brothers in a distant part
of the Kalahari. Masime, who had been the Silebe elder statesman,
lost influence after his elder brother's son, Mothibakgomo, became
head of the Silebe sub-clan. Moloise was a young man who had
aspired to influence, but who seemed to have lost his political standing,
at least temporarily, in 1966–7. During this period he was afflicted by
the loss of a child.

Mosonturi, who emerged as a leading political figure in 1966–7, was
a wealthy Ngologa from Lehututu who had established a cattle-post
in Kuli. He was staying there during the season of my visit and was
respected by everyone.

The total contribution of this category of citizens dropped consider-
ably between my two visits. I believe that this was inevitable, given
the sudden emergence of the District Councillor (who had not been
active in Kuli previously, since he came from the nearby village of
Nojane). Because the District Councillor took so prominent a part in
the deliberations of the *lekgota*, the more marginal village authorities
were displaced.

v

Taking the authorities as a group, can one see any common principles
behind their recruitment? It is clearly useful to be a close agnate of the
headman. In 1964, six of the eleven dominant citizens fell into this
category; and eight of the eleven in 1966–7. This is not, however, a
necessary or a sufficient condition of political prominence. Several of
the authorities have no agnatic connections with the headman, and
some of the headman's close agnates are not influential in political
affairs. The two younger sons of headman Ramoŝwane, who were
resident in Kuli during both my visits, play little part in politics.
Tsenene, Ramoŝwane's father's younger brother's son is also inactive,
although his sons are both members of the dominant group.

Secondly, representativeness is a factor in recruitment. Each of the
main political groupings in Kuli—the headman's supporters, Mabote's
faction and the Silebe—have members in the village authority. This

allows each grouping a voice in decision-making, and makes it possible to charge some men with specific responsibility on the village government's behalf for each sector of the village. However, there is no formal weighting of the membership of the inner circle of decision-makers (which is in any case an informal group). The most one can say is that there seems to be a tendency to include some representatives of each politically significant grouping in the village authority.

Thirdly, political and judicial ability are important. Several members of the village authority won prominence at least partly because they are 'good committee men'. I noted earlier that competence in political affairs is one of the qualifications for headmanship. It is demanded in all political positions, and its possession may override considerations of birth. Neither of the Silebe counsellors is particularly well-connected by kinship, nor are Tsenene's sons, Morimomongwe and Lebiki, much less the prominent independents, Waatotsi and Moloise. Affinal connections may be important, but in the case of all these men—as the villagers remark—influence came through 'speaking well in the council-place'.

Finally, the correlation between wealth and political influence is slight. The four wealthiest men in Kuli are the headman and his close agnates, Riphoni, Mabote and Tsenene. These men, or members of their family-groups, account for more than half the members of the village authority both in 1964 and 1966–7. This is chance, however. They are rich for the same reason as they are powerful—because they belong to the ruling line founded by Leswape I, who was a rich man. In some other villages the headman and his close agnates are not particularly wealthy. If one excepts these 'Sons of Leswape', the connection between wealth and influence in Kuli is less impressive. Some of the wealthy villagers, like Monantwe, have no political influence, while some of the influential men—Mokgethi, Modjathoši, Waatotsi and Moloise—are only moderately wealthy by village standards. Mokgetise, Mabote's younger brother, squandered his patrimony on the classic indulgences of wine and women, and though middle-aged, he lives as a dependent of his elder brother. Nevertheless, his political influence is strong.[1]

The recruitment of the District Councillor is influenced by rather special considerations. Luther Sakgu, who became District Councillor for Kuli, is a citizen of the nearby village of Nojane. He is a Ngologa,

---

[1] Wealth is measured mainly in terms of cattle-holdings, and the stock-holdings of Kuli citizens may be found in the Appendix.

and belongs to the Rakile clan, an off-shoot of the Pebana. He has distant affinal and matrilateral connections with the Kuli headman's family, and close agnatic connections with some minor figures in Kuli. His initial qualifications, then, are that although he comes from Nojane he is not in all senses an outsider; and yet he is not involved in any one of the kin-based factions in Kuli.

Luther also speaks good English, he is rich, well-known to the men of Kuli, and a man of influence in Nojane. Moreover, he was one of the District's political entrepreneurs, and in the immediate pre-independence period he was Jankie's closest associate, touring the District with him to promote the BDP's cause.

Both his position as a 'new man' of the District and his neutrality *vis-à-vis* the Kuli factions helped him to become District Councillor. His rival for the position was Leswape, the court-scribe, who was nominated by the village school-teacher and the District's representative in the Legislative Assembly. Leswape's candidature was attacked, firstly, on the grounds that headman Ramoŏwane 'just likes his own children'; and secondly on the basis that he would be less well able to cope with modern politics than Luther. Even some of the headman's close allies supported Luther's candidature, and after the *lekgota* had debated the nomination for some time, Mabote's faction and the Silebe came out strongly in Luther's favour. He was then chosen without a vote.

VI

If the District Councillor is detached from the village kin-based factions, most of the other members of the village authority are not. In fact, they provide the leadership of all the factions. Factionalism is endemic in the political life of the Sotho-speaking peoples.[1] In all Ngologa villages one finds at least two factions. One will be in support of the headman, the other often opposed to him. There may also be other factions, and there are usually a number of uncommitted citizens, some of whom may be members of the village authority.

As I have already described, Kuli has three factions—the two Pebana factions, one led by the headman, the other (an opposition group) led by one of his younger brothers, Mabote; and the Silebe faction. These factions are closely identified with co-residential and cooperative units within the village. Each has a basic core of two or three family-groups whose heads are close agnates, and a superstratum

[1] Casalis noted in Basutoland more than a century ago that 'Here, as everywhere, there is always a party for and a party against the government' (1861: 234).

of less closely attached allies, associated with the core group by residential proximity and also by ties of kinship and affinity.

In addition to these three factions, there are several politically uncommitted family-group heads. Some, like Waatotsi and Moloise, have considerable influence at times. Their lack of firm allegiance to any faction is connected with the fact that they do not have close agnatic connections to any group in the village. This cannot be said to determine their neutrality, however, for some faction members are also not members of the core agnatic units. These independents often intervene to break an impasse created by factional conflict, or to raise potentially embarrassing matters. They and high-status visitors (like Mosonturi) may have much the same catalytic role in village politics as has been noted for 'strangers' or 'outsiders' in other parts of the world.[1]

The factions within the ruling group crystallise on the death or succession of a headman. In Kuli, the conflict between Ramošwane and Mabote can be traced to the death of Leswape I and the fission of his family-group. Their opposition reached a peak in the late 1950s and early 1960s. The headman was accused of misusing village funds collected for a new village borehole, and his son Matlopelwe, who was then court-scribe and borehole pumper, was accused of irresponsibility and peculation, and after the intervention of the District Commissioner he lost his offices. During this crisis, Mabote's group was supported by the Silebe and egged on by the head-teacher, who was engaged on his own account in a series of court-cases against the headman and his family. He also wrote several times to the District Commissioner, complaining about the headman, Matlopelwe and Leswape. The District Commissioner then intervened for a second time and transferred the head-teacher, who became the scapegoat of the crisis. When I first came to Kuli, about a year after his transfer, he was spoken of with great virulence by men of all factions. When factional disputes took place, they were sometimes explained to me as a legacy of his machinations.

There is a tendency for two factions to polarise on particular types of political issue—briefly, those which involve jobs, which touch on long-standing quarrels, or which involve the power-structure of the village. The third faction, Mabote's or the Silebe sides with one group or the other, and their choice usually determines the outcome of the conflict.

---

[1] Frankenberg has paid special attention to this phenomenon, and in *Communities in Britain* (1966) he deals with examples from various British studies. I had the experience, shared by many anthropologists, of having to avoid being manoeuvred into this sort of position.

There are, however, a number of issues which do not provoke factional conflict, particularly legal matters, or issues in which the village confronts outside authorities. Moreover, the members of opposition factions are bound to the headman by ties which cross-cut factional differences, and they share an ideology which denies the legitimacy of factionalism. Leading members of Mabote's faction and of the Silebe group are popular counsellors, and so involved to some extent in the village government. Further, members of Mabote's faction, including Mabote himself, recognise the headman's claims as their senior patrikinsman. They also have affinal and matrilateral ties with the headman and leading members of his faction. Mabote once took pains to explain to me his matrilateral connection with the headman, who was also his paternal half-brother. He argued that this connection should have checked what he described as the headman's opposition to him. Several members of his faction complained to me that while they wish diligently to serve the headman, he insists on depending only on his son and grandson. These cross-cutting ties may at times even accentuate conflicts, but in general they work against the overt expression of opposition to the village government.

Finally, there are no established divisions within the village community along interest lines—rich *vs.* poor, educated *vs.* illiterate, or Christians *vs.* pagans. In Northern Kgalagadi District the national political parties provided the basis for a new expression of oppositions after Botswana's independence, but this has not happened in Ghanzi District. Some District Councillors have established pressure groups of 'progressive' citizens. These serve to advocate and clarify reforms, but where I have observed them they do not divide the citizen body or the authorities. In any case, there is no such group in Kuli. There is still a considerable measure of cultural unity, and villagers hold central values in common.

VII

The average Ngologa citizen attends *lekgota* meetings from time to time and sometimes makes a contribution to a debate. He is generally associated with one of the village factions, and he takes an interest in village politics. He or his brother or son may become members of the village authority if they demonstrate political ability. In many villages, however, there are groups of politically marginal men, who are not full members of the village community.

The degree to which political rights are enjoyed and exercised is an aspect of social distance which is often expressed in terms of a kinship idiom. It is important to be able to establish kinship relationships with villagers if one immigrates, preferably with members of the core agnatic corporation which founded the village. When one asks people why they moved from one village to another, they often say they came to join their kin. If one does not have kin in the ruling group or in another important section of the village, it is useful at least to be a member of the dominant tribal group. Villagers outside even this broad circle often have little to do with village politics—particularly if they live in a foreign enclave. On the other hand, an Ngologa on a visit from another village will participate freely in *lekgota* debates.

Herero and Nama Hottentot minorities, in particular, tend to form politically insignificant units in Tswana or Ngologa-ruled villages. In Lokgwabe the Hottentots constitute a semi-autonomous political unit within the village, which has little to do with the Ngologa majority. In Kalkfontein and Karakobis the small Herero communities regulate their own affairs by and large, and Herero seldom appear at meetings of the *lekgota*.

This political distancing is correlated with cultural variation. The Tswana and Ngologa are culturally cognate, and each behaves more like a sub-clan than a foreign community in a village ruled by the other. The Herero, however, belong to the distinct Western Bantu cultural complex, and the Nama are even further removed by language and tradition. Intermarriage is also rare across these cultural barriers. (There is little feeling that these other groups are inferior to one's own, although the Tswana do tend to look down on all Kgalagari.)

In Kuli the Bushmen are the only minority, and as I indicated earlier, they are a special case. The Bushmen are altogether outside the political fold—'lesser breeds without the Law'. They have no civil rights except those they can secure *ad hoc* through the direct intervention of Government officers. Further, a true marriage—with the passing of bride-wealth—is unheard of between a Bantu villager and a Bushman.

VIII

Summary

It may be useful at this stage to make a brief, coherent statement on the main features of the village political structure and its context, summing up the argument so far.

The Kalahari headman has never been very powerful, and despite the advent of overrule he remains dependent on the support of the majority of his subjects. The effective decision-making body in the village is a group within the *lekgota* which I call the village authority. In Kuli the authorities represent the main elements of the political body and include all the office-holders, but recruitment is weighted in favour of the 'Sons of Leswape'. The village authority is not a cohesive body, and on many issues it splits into factions, each faction drawing some support from ordinary citizens.

These factions are based on groupings which are generated and ordered within a matrix of kinship relationships. The three factions in Kuli correspond broadly to co-residential alliances, with various social and economic functions, which are structured about patrilineal cores and cemented by ongoing ties of kinship and affinity.

The village is the basic unit of District Administration, which is headed by the District Commissioner. Communication between the village and the District Administration is poor, and although it has improved since 1966, the District Commissioner may still make crucial decisions without reference to the demands of the villagers. The improvements in communication and the progress which has been made in consultation, are largely the result of the institutionalisation of the role of the District's 'new men' since Botswana's independence. As District Councillors, these 'new men' are beginning to close the gap between the District Administration and the village, and in the process they have acquired considerable influence within the villages. They have generally supplanted the headman and court-scribes as the main institutionalised channels of communication with external agencies on a wide range of issues, and they have taken over the leadership of the *lekgota* when problems of 'modernisation' are under consideration.

6

THE STUFF OF POLITICS

I

The *lekgota* normally meets once or twice a week, slightly more frequently in large than in small villages. The meetings usually begin in the late morning, when the cattle and goats have been watered, and may last for anything from an hour and a half to five hours or more. Meetings always break up before sunset, and if the business of the day has not been completed, another meeting may be called soon after to deal with it. A series of meetings may be held if an urgent matter is to be settled, or if the District Commissioner is due to visit the village; but at other times *lekgota* sessions may be postponed because some of the authorities are absent, or because a bridewealth ceremony is being held, or for some other reason. Attendance falls off during the seasons of peak agricultural activity, but the *lekgota* continues to meet fairly frequently.

The Ngologa distinguish between a meeting called to hear an action at law (*tsheko*) from other types of *lekgota* session—called *pijo*. A debate is similarly classified as a *tsheko*, a legal matter, or a *puo*, some other public issue. A *lekgota* session may, however, pass from a law suit to a debate on policy, and at any meeting a diverse range of public concerns may be aired.

Table 5 on pages 93–9 sets out the business debated by the Kuli *lekgota* at thirty-one meetings held during my stay in 1964, and ten meetings which I recorded in 1966–7.

Table 5. *Business transacted at meetings of the Kuli* lekgota

No.	Date	Called at the instance of	Business transacted
1.	30/1/64	District Commissioner	(a) Projected census discussed.
			(b) Constitution for self-government outlined, explained and discussed.
			(c) Cattle-export problems discussed.
			(d) Some citizens complain about the headman; they want a younger man.

No.	Date	Called at the instance of	Business transacted
			(*e*) Possible expansion of village school requested and discussed.
			(*f*) Question of inadequate village water-supply raised; a second bore-hole requested from Government.
2.	18/2/64	Headman	(*a*) Messages from DC★ read.
			(*b*) BDP village organisation discussed; administrative assistance requested.
			(*c*) Counsellor reprimanded by head-man for missing some *lekgota* sessions; headman wants to fine him.
			(*d*) Assault case discussed but not settled.
3.	19/2/64	Headman	(*a*) Question of fining counsellor discussed again (see 2*c*).
			(*b*) General issue of poor attendance at *lekgota* meetings discussed.
			(*c*) Two cases called but not tried; protagonists are absent.
			(*d*) Maltreatment of Bushmen discussed.
			(*e*) Issue of defaulting on taxes and court-fines raised.
4.	19/2/64	BDP (meeting commenced immediately after no. 3)	(*a*) Party politics and leading national politicians discussed.
			(*b*) National party news reviewed.
			(*c*) A more humane treatment of Bushmen, in keeping with BDP ideology, discussed.
5.	26/2/64	Headman and teachers	(*a*) Complaints from the two village schoolteachers concerning the condition of the school-house, teachers' accommodation, fees, attendance and parent-teacher relations discussed, and measures proposed to meet the complaints.
6.	10/4/64	BDP	(*a*) BDP annual congress described and some of the issues raised there explained and discussed.
7.	13/4/64	Headman	(*a*) Messages from DC read and discussed.
			(*b*) Overdue fines demanded.
			(*c*) Agreement reached to raise a levy for school building; citizens urged to send cattle to forthcoming sale to raise money.
			(*d*) Court-scribe criticised for reporting to DC that a number of men were overdue with their fines.

No.	Date	Called at the instance of	Business transacted
			(e) Local Bushmen leaders summoned and instructed to join the BDP.
8.	21/4/64	Headman	(a) Overdue fines discussed again and offenders urged to pay (see 7 b).
			(b) Messages from DC read and discussed.
			(c) Letter read from Nojane head-teacher complaining of absenteeism among Kuli schoolchildren there; problems of children attending Nojane school discussed.
			(d) Kuli schoolteachers raise their complaints once more (see 5 a).
9.†	25/4/64	Cattle-guard	(a) Cattle-guard complains about mal-treatment of livestock and brings an action against a citizen which is heard.
10.†	18/5/64	Headman	(a) Counsellors report on a meeting called by the DC in Ghanzi; and on the subsequent unofficial meet-ing of prominent African villagers to consider African grievances.
11.†	16/6/64	Headman	(a) A case concerning a dispute about a sale of cattle heard and settled.
12.†	13/7/64	Headman	(a) Another dispute arising out of sale of livestock heard.
13.	21/7/64	Headman	(a) Levies for school building and a new reservoir for borehole dis-cussed (see 7 c).
			(b) Letter from DC read.
14.	23/7/64	Headman	(a) New tax on cattle-sales announced and discussed.
			(b) Levies on school building and bore-hole discussed (see 7 c and 13 a).
			(c) Possible measures against citizens who have not paid court-fines discussed (see 7 b and 8 a).
15.	25/7/64	District Commissioner	(a) Voting procedure in forthcoming election explained.
			(b) Revision of tax-register discussed.
			(c) Cattle-sales discussed.
			(d) Government plan for food hand-outs for schoolchildren discussed.
			(e) Food for destitutes promised by Government, and also temporary relaxation of hunting restrictions, in view of prevailing drought.
			(f) Village water-supply and projected borehole discussed (see 1 f).

No.	Date	Called at the instance of	Business transacted
15. (*contd.*)			(*g*) Transport difficulties and postal delays reported.
			(*h*) Citizens complain about Bushmen stock-theft.
16.	29/7/64	Headman	(*a*) Assault case tried.
17.	3/8/64	Headman	(*a*) Outstanding court-fines demanded (see 7 *b*, 8 *a* and 14 *c*).
			(*b*) Complaints heard from the pumper in charge of the village borehole, and his appointment and terms of service confirmed.
18.†	12/8/64	Headman	(*a*) Two men who persisted in non-payment of court-fines whipped by a counsellor in the presence of a police-officer (see 7 *b*, 8 *a*, 14 *c* and 17 *a*).
19.	20/8/64	Headman	(*a*) Trial and sentence of Bushman stock-thieves.
20.	21/8/64	Headman	(*a*) Messages from DC and BDP read.
			(*b*) Theft case tried.
21.	7/9/64	Headman	(*a*) A register of the destitutes in the village drawn up and applicants for Government destitute relief questioned.
22.	9/9/64	District Commissioner	(*a*) Regulations for voter-registration reviewed.
			(*b*) Forthcoming visit of agricultural officer announced.
			(*c*) Feeding of destitutes discussed.
23.	15/11/64	Headman	(*a*) Coming visit of DC announced; discussion of questions which should be put to him.
			(*b*) Progress of school-building levy reviewed, and citizens urged to contribute (see 7 *c*, 13 *a* and 14 *b*).
			(*c*) Arrangements made to try two cases.
24.	17/11/64	Headman	(*a*) Issues to be raised at DC's meeting with *lekgota* settled upon (see 23 *a*).
			(*b*) School-building levy discussed again (see 7 *c*, 13 *a*, 14 *b* and 23 *b*).
			(*c*) An old lady presents a suit for damages, and it is agreed to give her a hearing.
			(*d*) Pumper complains about non-payment of his wages; debate (see 17 *b*).
25.	17/11/64	District Commissioner (meeting began immediately after no. 24)	(*a*) DC announces he has been transferred and makes farewell speech.

No.	Date	Called at the instance of	Business transacted
			(b) Registration of voters discussed.
			(c) Expansion of school agreed to by Government; size of levy reduced (see 1 e, 7 c, 13 a, 14 b, 23 b and 24 b).
			(d) Further discussion of water problems and possibility of a supplementary borehole (see 1 f and 15 f).
			(e) DC appealed to and endorses pumper's wage-claim (see 17 b and 24 d).
26.	19/11/64	Headman	(a) Collection of money to buy supplies of dieseline for borehole discussed.
			(b) Case of disputed sale tried (see 12 a).
27.	30/11/64	Headman	(a) Encroachment of villagers from Nojane on Kuli grazing and watering areas discussed.
			(b) Case of damages postponed due to illness of protagonists (see 24 c).
			(c) Visit of veterinary officer announced.
28.	1/12/64	Veterinary officer	(a) Organisation of a cattle-drive to Lobatsi abattoir discussed.
29.	3/12/64	BDP	(a) Nominations for District BDP chairmanship and electoral candidate discussed; Kuli citizens make their choices and nominate delegates to the local convention which will choose the men for these positions.
30.	28/12/64	Headman	(a) Delegates report back on District BDP convention and nominations (see 29 a).
			(b) They then report on another meeting they attended, called by the Resident Commissioner at Ghanzi, where the country's future was discussed.
			(c) They then report on a third meeting, with the veterinary officer, who discussed with them developments in the organisation of the projected cattle-drive (see 28 a).‡
			(d) Development of school discussed (see 1 e, 7 c, 13 a, 14 b, 23 b and 24 b).
			(e) Possibility of establishing Ngologa hegemony in Nojane discussed; Nojane people should be made to pay taxes in Kuli.
			(f) Conflict over purchase of dieseline for borehole temporarily resolved (see 26 a).

No.	Date	Called at the instance of	Business transacted
30. (*contd.*)			(*g*) An old lady brings two cases, which are discussed.
31.	30/12/64	Headman	(*a*) The headman enquires into the smuggling of cattle into South West Africa: some village youths have been arrested there.
			(*b*) Case of disputed sale: judgment not yet executed (see 12 *a* and 26 *b*).
			(*c*) Case of damages settled (see 24 *c* and 27 *b*).
32.	10/10/66	District Councillor	(*a*) *Ipelegeng* ('Food for work') project in village discussed.
			(*b*) Non-payment for school-books remarked.
			(*c*) Expenditure on Independence celebrations reported.
33.	28/10/66	District Councillor	(*a*) *Ipelegeng* programme discussed (see 32 *a*).
			(*b*) Castration of inferior male stock urged.
			(*c*) New tax-payers registered.
			(*d*) Complaints made about lack of village store; possibility of a co-operative mooted.
			(*e*) Repeated complaint on non-payment for school-books (see 32 *b*).
			(*f*) Dispute over operation of borehole arises again, and is debated (see 17 *b*, 24 *d*, 25 *e*, 26 *a* and 30*f*).
			(*g*) Questions raised and answered about legal status of *matimela* (stray) cattle and goats.
			(*h*) Problem of excessive drinking by women discussed.
			(*i*) Case of Bushman stock-theft set down.
34.	4/11/66	Headman	(*a*) Bushman thieves tried; case not concluded (see 33*i*).
			(*b*) Announced that village must raise a storeroom for the school-feeding scheme.
			(*c*) Forthcoming supply of seed by Government announced.
			(*d*) Forthcoming TB vaccination programme announced.
35.	18/11/66	District Commissioner	(*a*) Introduction of European District Councillors, with whom District Commissioner is making a tour.

No.	Date	Called at the instance of	Business transacted
36.	12/1/67	Headman	(*a*) Assault case tried. (*b*) Case of breach of contract reported. (*c*) Case of damage to property reported.
37.	14/1/67	Headman	(*a*) Preliminary investigation of Bushman stock-theft, in presence of police-officer.
38.	3/2/67	Vice-President of Botswana	(*a*] The Vice-President addressed the *lekgota*, urging progressive farming and other desiderata; he then fielded a number of questions from citizens, covering a number of Government policies, and in particular the new, higher school-fees.
39.	11/2/67	District Councillor	(*a*) New watering fees discussed. (*b*) Government suggestion that police be posted in the villages announced and discussed. (*c*) Complaints made about racial discrimination in the District. (*d*) District Council debate on territorial dispute (over Tšukudu pan) discussed. (*e*) Applications for permits to work in South West Africa collected. (*f*) Forthcoming visit of DC announced; it is agreed that outstanding cases should be heard before his arrival. (*g*) Date for cattle-sale announced; policy for sellers discussed. (*h*) Case raised, but postponed.
40.	18/3/67	Headman's deputy	(*a*) Preliminary hearing of breach of contract case; trial postponed.
41.	24/3/67	Headman	(*a*) DC's demand for outstanding fines and taxes communicated. (*b*) Further postponement of case (see 39 *h*).

⋆ DC = District Commissioner and BDP = Botswana Democratic Party.

† Meetings at which I was not present, and which were reported upon by the court-scribe.

‡ This particular cattle-drive never took place: among other things, because the veterinary officer was transferred.

The business dealt with by the *lekgota* may be classified in various ways, but some sort of pattern can be remarked. In roughly one-fifth of all issues the *lekgota* acts simply as a passive recipient of instructions or information from Government officers, or the Democratic Party. These are usually routine matters, and the *lekgota* can do little to affect the situation. In over a fifth of cases, however, issues introduced by these external authorities do generate political activity—for example, the Democratic Party's requests for nominations to various offices; or the District Commissioner's demands for outstanding fines which had been ordered by the *lekgota*. This aspect of the *lekgota*'s business was naturally influenced by the fact that during much of my time in the Kalahari, Botswana was preparing for independence, and at the same time was suffering from a severe drought. Hence the concern for the census, voting procedures, nominations of candidates; and also the arrangements for famine-relief, culminating in the *Ipelegeng* programme.

Over half of the *lekgota*'s business is concerned mainly with domestic issues, although here too the outside authorities may intervene. About a fifth of the issues recorded are legal. About a third deal with the major public utilities, the school and the borehole, or with the main source of other aspects of domestic administration and the exercise of authority, and demands of various kinds from citizens.

The simple distribution of issues dealt with by the *lekgota* is not an accurate reflection of the importance of the issues for the citizens, or of the time devoted to various sorts of business. A single law-suit may take several hours, occupying an entire session of the *lekgota*, while routine communications from the District Commissioner may be dealt with in a few minutes. The balance of the issues involve wealth, cattle, in one way or another. Matters in which the *lekgota* has authority account for most of the time spent in debate.

II

The work of the *lekgota* as a court may with advantage be considered separately. It is the central court of the village and enjoys Government recognition and support. (I shall be dealing later with the subsidiary village courts, which arbitrate sectional disputes or carry out preparatory examinations.)

I was able to copy the court-records of Kuli, Kalkfontein and Hukuntsi—the latter a special case, since it deals with appeals from the other village courts in Matseng as well as its own matters, and is more concerned than the other village courts with statutory offences. In Kuli these records are intermittently preserved for the period 1946–67, and include ninety-eight cases which between them involved 112 issues. The Kalkfontein records are complete for the period August 1962 to December 1966, and cover 111 cases. Unfortunately, the record of twenty-four of these cases is totally inadequate, and I was therefore able to identify only ninety-seven of the issues with which this court dealt.

Table 6 sets out the distribution of the issues dealt with in the courts of Kuli and Kalkfontein. In Table 7, I compare the overall pattern of distribution of the issues in these two villages.[1]

Table 6. *Classification by issue of cases recorded in the courts of Kuli and Kalkfontein*

Issue	No.	% of all issues
PRIVATE DELICTS	[152]	[74]
Assault	66	32
Theft and robbery	45	22
Damage to property	12	6
Seduction and paternity	12	6
Adultery	9	4
Insult and defamation	8	4
PUBLIC DELICTS	[22]	[10]
Contempt of court	7	3
Political misdemeanours	6	3
Obstructing the course of justice	3	1
Statutory and miscellaneous	6	3
FAMILY LAW	19	9
CONTRACTS	11	5
PROPERTY	5	2
Total	209	100%

The distribution of issues in Kuli is very similar to that in Kalk-fontein, and indeed both parallel the distribution of issues recorded for Tswana courts by Schapera.[2] Private delicts account for nearly three-quarters of all issues, and assault, theft and robbery alone account for over half of all issues. In other words, the bulk of the work of the *lekgota* as a court is concerned with the protection of person and property from attacks of one kind or another. Only 16 per cent of all cases are concerned with conflicting claims on persons or property (i.e. cases of Family Law, Property and Contracts. If one includes cases of adultery, seduction and paternity under this head, the proportion

[1] For further information (including some material on the Hukuntsi court) see my paper, 'The Work of Customary Courts . . .' (1969).

[2] Schapera (1943). The paper also provides the model for my classification of issues.

8

Table 7. *Percentage distribution of issues in the
courts of Kuli and Kalkfontein*

Issue	Kuli	Kalkfontein
Private delicts	70	76
Public delicts	11	10
Family law	10	8
Contracts	5	5
Property	4	1
Total	100	100

rises to 26 per cent). Political cases, or offences against the village government (public delicts) account for an even smaller proportion, 10 per cent of all issues dealt with.

In some cases which are brought by an injured party the court may intervene and impose a retributive sanction in addition to, or instead of, restitution. Both parties may even be punished, as when both the appellant and defendant in an assault case are found to have misbehaved. One might quibble about whether such cases should be classified as public or private delicts, but this sort of intervention by the court is rare in practice, except in assault cases. One should note, however, that the court may intervene on behalf of the community in any case if public order and morality have been infringed.

A final point of great importance concerns the parties involved in litigation. Litigants are normally male citizens, and in the overwhelming majority of cases they are not close agnates. Rights in persons and property are vested in men, and these men are members of agnatic corporations. The corporation is a jural personality, and therefore disputes between members cannot be dealt with satisfactorily by the court. Only about 6 per cent of the cases dealt with by the Kuli *lekgota* involved close agnates. On the other hand, rights over women are often vaguely defined and may be a source of dispute. About 18 per cent of the Kuli cases pitted affines against one another.

III

The use of the *lekgota* as a court, to settle disputes, particularly between members of different family-groups, and to maintain the law (*molao*) is stressed by the Ngologa. They also use the political machinery to pursue economic aims—in which I include their educational aims, which are seen as yielding primarily economic rewards. Finally the political institutions are, of course, used for administrative purposes, and they are the locus of conflicts over jobs and competition for influence on decision-making. The economic and strictly political interests of the Ngologa warrant further discussion here.

The modern Ngologa depend for cash mainly on the use and sale of livestock and livestock products, although they sometimes go on migrant labour to find ready cash or to build up stock-holdings. Food is provided by the agricultural work of the women and by some hunting and gathering. There is no shortage of land, and little political activity is generated by their agricultural activities. Livestock, on the other hand, particularly cattle, are a perpetual concern of the men.

The cattle-owner wants water, grazing, good markets, and security from thieves and predators. Security from predators is never a contentious matter, and a headman can usually find on his own authority some adventurous hunters who will deal with a lion that has formed a taste for beef. Stock-theft in the Kalahari is always blamed on Bushmen. When they are caught the police deal with them, or pass them on to the village court for action. If the thief is the serf of a citizen, his master may make good the loss, but normally there is no possibility of compensation. The Ngologa recognise that punitive action is not enough—particularly in bad years, Bushmen will steal. Occasionally they face the social roots of the problem and moot new approaches to the Bushmen in the *lekgota*: discipline them even more strongly; help them or assimilate them; demand stronger protection from Government, etc. Their pressure on Government has not been without effect, although no radical measures have been taken to deal with this problem.

Water and grazing rights involve, first, grants of citizenship or temporary permission to water and graze stock in a particular area. This implies that the village authorities are able to exercise claims over a defined territory, and that they must weigh various claims from groups inside and outside the community.

The single most valued resource is water, and while the amount of grazing is more or less fixed, the available water supply can be increased—most efficiently by sinking boreholes. The initial investment is large and risky, for a borehole may fail; and the cost of upkeep is high. Sometimes rich men from different groups in the village combine to acquire a borehole, but more usually only the village as a whole can afford to pay for boreholes, or persuade Government to supply them. The vital importance of the borehole combined with the difficulties involved in acquiring and administering them, give rise to a great deal of political activity. Kalahari boreholes are frequently the centre of bitter and prolonged political conflicts, as will be seen later.

Problems of marketing cattle are largely dealt with outside the political arena, for the villagers can exert practically no influence, even through the District Commissioner, on the big buyers. Until recently, the best they could do was persuade the District Commissioner to arrange a market at a convenient place and time. For the rest, whether one sold cattle through orthodox channels or smuggled them into South West Africa, and similar decisions, were a matter of personal choice. Recently, however, cooperatives have been set up, aimed mainly at organising largescale drives to the faraway Lobatsi abattoir. These enterprises normally involve the use of the village political machinery, if only for purposes of discussion.

Most villages have a store, usually run by a European or Indian trader, to which they sell hides and skins and, when things are tight, cattle. (Kuli has no store, but the villagers buy and sell at the store in nearby Nojane.) The District Commissioner is often urged to persuade traders to give the people more favourable terms, and, recently, to grant trading and hawking licences to Africans. Boycotts have never been organised, however, and it is only since Independence that buying and selling cooperatives have been started.

Veterinary services for livestock, seeds for agriculture and permits for migrant labour are provided by Government. The villagers may use their political machinery to apply pressure on the District authorities, but by and large they are relegated to an administrative role in these fields, publicising the services and arranging for the distribution of the goods. Hunting rights are similarly controlled by Government, and although they may be extended in bad years, it is beyond the power of the villagers to effect the abrogation of all restrictions. In some cases village authorities have circumscribed trapping, when it has interfered with the safety of livestock.

Rights in women, children and Bushmen serfs also have their economic dimension. While conflicts over such rights are generally regulated through legal channels, the question of Bushmen serfs has become a political issue. The villagers are extremely concerned about their weakening control over Bushmen, but the large political and social forces which will, in the long run, determine the position of the Bushmen, are beyond their control. They do, however, feel the impact of Government's tardy and still somewhat reluctant concern for the

Bushmen, and frequently complain that while 'Bushmen now belong to Government', Government does nothing about them, even when they steal.

The Ngologa regard schools as an investment, since educated children will command large salaries as migrant labourers, and can help to administer the increasingly complex financial affairs of their parents. Moreover, educated citizens are better able to tackle the political forces outside the village than their illiterate elders, and so in the long run, they will help further the interests of the villagers. The series of political issues generated by their concern with schooling include the problems of raising levies and labour to extend schools and teachers' quarters, the maintenance of regular attendance, and the payment of fees and purchase of books. The immediate goal is the extension of locally available services. The danger is that Government may block expansion, or withdraw teachers from the higher grades, or increase fees. The provision and maintenance of physical facilities is left partly to the villagers, and their success in providing them is one test used by Government in allocating resources. For the rest, the villagers may do their best to keep the school going, but they cannot effectively influence the major decisions concerning the allocation of educational facilities.

The Ngologa are keenly political, and there is often bitter conflict over the allocation of jobs by the village government, and competition for influence in the *lekgota*. The interests behind these political activities are sometimes difficult to fathom. Some of the jobs are not economically rewarding, and many key economic interests are shared and pursued collectively. Nor is there much to be gained from controlling the legal machinery, since it cannot be bent regularly to the interests of one group without being disrupted. Intra-village and ethnic political conflicts are best understood if they are related to structural oppositions within the social system; to attempt to trace them to material interests alone is probably misguided.

It should also be stressed that there is a common interest in maintaining the political and more especially the legal structure. Legal matters are characterised by the unanimity of members of the court, and the villagers combine and submerge sectional interests if there is a threat to the *molao*. The law is only occasionally used to further the interests of the majority, and this is possible only in multi-tribal villages with ethnic minorities. (In Hukuntsi the sub-chief, backed by the police, has been able to use the law to maintain his own authority against opposition. This is a unique situation, however.)

To sum up, vital economic interests are shared and pressed unitedly (though on balance ineffectively) on outside powers, mainly the Government. The political machinery is also used to administer policies initiated from outside for economic and political development, and (especially since Independence) to organise joint economic action. Within the village, people unite to defend the integrity of the political system and to apply the law, but divide in competition for jobs and influence.

IV

I have been concerned with the range of affairs which the Ngologa deal with through their political institutions. To round out the picture, it is worthwhile to consider briefly what is *excluded* from the political domain of action.

First of all, the affairs of the family-group members are rarely brought before the public institutions. They are dealt with by domestic arbitration or by other non-political processes; for example, accusations that malignant magic is being employed (consciously or unconsciously), which may lead to group fission. Minors and Bushmen serfs are regarded as, in a sense, the property of the group members, and if they conflict this is also normally treated as a private affair. (The position of married women is more complex than that of other minors, and I shall consider it later.) Where an association of family-groups forms a solidary unit, it also becomes an enclave within the political society. The domestic domain expands at the expense of the political.

Secondly, the churches are not integrated into the political system, but rather supplement it in certain areas of social life. The internal affairs of the churches are normally outside the purview of the political authority, and certain matters which are dealt with by the political institutions in other societies are here referred to the religious bodies for action. The headman is often the patron of a church, but he is not usually the leader of the congregation. The churches have even taken over some (perhaps never very important) religious functions of the headman. Traditionally the headman was a rain-maker, but while he is now expected to find rain-makers on behalf of the community (religious leaders or Bushmen), his responsibility goes no further.

The separation of political and religious activities became even more evident in the course of the drought of the early 1960s. The village authorities turned to Government for assistance. At the same time, neo-Christian prophets emerged, who diagnosed the causes of the natural calamity in magical terms. They attempted to restore prosperity by organising rain-making ceremonies, prayer meetings, anti-witch drives, etc., throughout the country.[1] These prophets usually worked with the permission of the headmen—sometimes at their invitation—but they were outside the political system, and made no attempt to use it or change it.

In short, domestic and religious groups complement the activity of the political institutions in the regulation of certain areas of social life, and both normally manage their internal affairs without resort to the political machinery of the village. Each is characterised by a set of values which is distinct from the system of values contained within the political system itself.

Thirdly, Ngologa politics is the business of men. The affairs of women are normally dealt with only to the extent that the rights of men, as husbands, fathers or brothers, are involved. Even then, the political institutions will take notice only if men from different family-groups are brought into conflict. This is fairly common, for the transfer of rights in marriage is a lengthy and inconclusive process. Two family-groups—and, given the enterprise of Ngologa women, sometimes three—may be involved in a marital dispute.

As a rule, only a man can initiate a political or legal issue, although he may do so on behalf of a woman under his care. If an older woman becomes a household head and is involved in a dispute, the political authorities may have no alternative but to hear her suit, but they will do so with reluctance and will stress the anomolous nature of the situation.

In addition to these internal limitations of the village political field, there are constraints imposed from above, or resulting from social changes of various kinds. Some traditionally political matters are neglected by the modern Ngologa; in some cases they believe that their interest can no longer be safely indulged. A good example is the disappearance of initiation ceremonies, and the neglect of the age-sets, once a major area of village governmental activity. The causes are several: the belief that Government is against initiation ceremonies; the growth of migrant labour and the disinclination of the young men

---

[1] The prophets (*maporofiti*) were not Ngologa or Tswana. The two leading figures were both Herero, and a Hottentot in Kalkfontein had some success in gaining acceptance. They organised local congregations, which briefly incorporated the churches which already existed, but this incipient organisation never became established. Already in 1964 the influence of the prophets was on the wane, and by 1966 they had faded away, with the partial exception of the prophet of Karakobis.

for these traditional disciplines; and the rise of Government schools. Other matters, such as action against witches or sorcerers, have been excluded from the purview of the village court by Government.

Finally, there is a range of affairs which may concern the villagers but which it is beyond the power of the village authorities to influence. The most important of these concern the organisation and allocation of national or District resources. The villagers are seldom seriously consulted about such matters, although the accomplished decisions may be communicated to the villagers, in the form of a request for action, or simply as information, and sometimes there is a degree of feed-back. To that extent, such issues may be defined as marginally political from the standpoint of the villagers. Participation in high-level decision-making increased slightly as Botswana moved towards independence, notably after the formation of District Councils in 1966. Nevertheless, the villagers are still largely excluded from effective participation in these processes.

v

In the following chapters, I shall be concerned with the process by which political and legal issues are dealt with. Different sorts of issue generate different types of decision-making process, and three main categories may be distinguished:

(a) *Legal issues:* involve the settlement of disputes between men of different family-groups over conflicting rights, or resulting from attacks on person or property. The case is normally brought by a citizen. It is assessed with the help of witnesses, judged against a code of law and precedents, and resolved by an order of restitution, or a punishment, or both. The *lekgota* is typically internally united, and detached from both parties.

(b) *Domestic political issues:* involve competition within the village between men of different (but structurally equivalent) groups, to control the decision-making machinery and the personal rewards of village politics. These issues are thrashed out in terms of the interests of the community, or segments within it, without any objective guide-lines (except purely procedural ones), and effective decisions can be reached only if the minority submits.

(c) *External political issues:* involve the pursuit of communal interests with respect to Government or other communities. In matters of this sort, the villagers are usually united, but often unable to affect the course of events.

This is not, of course, a water-tight classification. Some administrative issues might be classified in different ways, and a single issue may present itself in various forms at different times. An external political issue, for example, may generate domestic disputes, and a legal issue may have domestic or external political overtones. In the following chapter, I deal with domestic and external policy issues, and then, in Chapter 8, I consider legal decision-making and the administration of the law.

7

POLICY-MAKING AND ADMINISTRATION

The headman and other members of the village government may take some routine administrative decisions on their own, but no major decision is taken without consulting the *lekgota*. Indeed, with the exception of some matters which are settled by the direct intervention of external authorities, no decision is enforceable unless it is supported by general consensus. The policy-making process is therefore perforce highly democratic, unless the external authorities are directly involved.

At the same time, the image of decision-making is hierarchical—the people will say that the counsellors solicit the advice of the citizen body, but guide them, and that the headman is at last simply 'prayed' to concede the popular view. The formal hierarchy and actual democracy combine to shape the decision-making process. An issue is presented to the meeting by the chief counsellor, or sometimes a popular counsellor, speaking for the headman. The citizens debate the matter, led by the village authorities, and gradually a consensus emerges—or fails to emerge. This stage of the debate generally occupies the longest period of time, and it is characterised by free and forceful exchanges of opinion. The feeling of the meeting is then formulated by a popular counsellor, who 'prays' the chief counsellor. He in turn outlines the situation to the headman, who states the final decision, which is usually in line with the consensus.

This combination of hierarchy and democracy finds a parallel in the mixture of formality and informality which characterises Ngologa behaviour in the council-place (*kgota*). The *kgota* is a physically distinct arena, often fenced off with high poles, in a central part of the village. It is a place of the men, but a place in which even men observe special rules, particularly when the *lekgota* is in session. One may not bring a stick or any other weapon into the *kgota*; and one should be sober and decently dressed when in attendance. One may not smoke during meetings. When speaking, one stands and removes one's hat—only the headman may address the *lekgota* with his head covered. The headman and the members of the village government generally sit on chairs, while other citizens sit on the ground (though they may bring chairs along for themselves if they wish to do so).

Yet despite these conventions, the informality and freedom of expression is remarkable. Visitors accustomed to the greater orderliness of council meetings in the large Tswana capitals are often shocked, but the contrast simply reflects the contrast between the authority of the Tswana chief and the greater dependence on his people of the Ngologa headman. People carry on private discussions while someone is making an impassioned speech. Interjections are tolerated; speakers are heckled; and there is always ready laughter. Periodically, men leave the meeting to have a smoke outside the *kgota*, to relieve themselves, or perhaps to shout orders to children or to Bushmen serfs.

These oppositions between the village headman and the citizens, between hierarchy and democracy, and between formality and informality, are, however, only some of the dimensions of the decision-making process in the *lekgota*. I shall be more concerned in this and the following chapters with the distinctions between the judicial process and policy-making, and, where policy-making is concerned, between decisions made primarily in a domestic context, and those in which the determining powers rest with outside authorities. Conflict is particularly likely when the effective decision is in the hands of the villagers; and the villagers are most united when pressing demands on Government.

In this chapter, I explore the manner in which decisions on matters of policy are reached and executed. (The judicial process and the administration of the law is dealt with in the following chapter.) I begin with decisions which involve the villagers with the District Administration, and move on to decisions which are more directly the responsibility of the villagers. This parallels the shift from consensus to open conflict.

I have already indicated the impact of the District Councillor and other post-Independence developments on village affairs. The first series of cases, collected in 1964, deal with the pre-Independence situation. I shall then set out some cases which illustrate the changes I found in 1966–7.

II

Sometimes the headman is simply instructed to carry out a Government policy in a particular fashion. For example, the District Commissioner may write to tell him that a new tax has been levied on all cattle-sales, and that this must be collected by the court-scribe. When this particular tax was announced, the villagers reacted strongly. They complained about the court-scribe's immediate implementation of the tax, and they protested to the District Commissioner when he next made a tour of the District. They knew, however, that the decision had been taken at the national level, and that they could do nothing about it.

To take another example, when, in 1964, some small-scale famine-relief was organised by Government for people designated as destitute, the headman was instructed to compile a list of such people in his village, and to distribute among them the food which was later provided. The criteria of destitution were laid down by Government, and officials later inspected the way in which the orders had been interpreted and executed.

In some cases the villagers may be able to press their demands, even though the decision will be taken at District or national level. This is particularly true where the District Commissioner has latitude in the allocation of resources. Examples are school expansion, water development, the local relaxation of hunting restrictions, the provision of seeds, and the organisation of markets. The villagers are usually solidly united in their demands, and these are put to the District Commissioner by letter or when he meets the *lekgota* in the village.

The villagers are equally united when faced with a challenge from outsiders for watering rights or grazing, or with disputes about territory or hegemony. Nowadays, these disputes are sorted out, if at all, by the District authorities. In the past, a joint *lekgota* session might have been held, and occasionally violence erupted.

III

Although the villagers may have occasional successes as a pressure group within the District, they are generally impotent in 'external relations'. However, some policies which are initiated by central Government or at District level demand the participation of the villagers, and this may necessitate subsidiary policy-making at the village level.

The pattern is generally as follows: the villagers press a particular demand on the District authorities (or respond favourably to an initiative from above); when the District authorities are in a position to meet the demand, they require the villagers to share the administrative and financial burdens; the villagers then have to agree on how they should meet their commitment.

Two issues of this kind preoccupied the Kuli *lekgota* in 1964: the improvement of the water resources of the village; and the extension of the village school. These issues were raised whenever the District Commissioner visited the village, and some joint action was organised. A description of the debates on the extension of the school facilities will illustrate this type of policy-making.

The expansion of the school

The village school in Kuli had gradually been built up until it was giving instruction up to Standard IV (i.e. six years of primary education). Then, after a long conflict between the headman and the head-teacher, which ended with the transfer of the latter, the school was downgraded and permitted only to give four years of primary education. Those children at Kuli who wished to complete their primary education were obliged to attend the Nojane school, about twelve miles away. This arrangement was unsatisfactory, for there were no boarding facilities at Nojane and food was scarce. The children complained that they were uncomfortable and hungry at Nojane, and several withdrew from the school despite parental opposition.

The villagers were united in deploring the situation and in their desire for education for their children. The headman expressed the general feeling when he told the *lekgota*: 'Children must be sent to school. The school protects the village. I want children to attend the school.' The obvious solution was to upgrade the Kuli school to its previous level.[1]

Early in 1964, the District Commissioner told the Kuli *lekgota* that he had money in hand for educational expansion. He said that he was prepared to build an additional classroom in Kuli, supply another teacher, and restore Standard IV instruction, on condition that the villagers showed their active interest. This interest should be manifested by raising attendance at the school, and by making contributions to the cost and labour required to raise another classroom. He concluded by promising that if the villagers collected R200, Government would meet the remaining costs.

The villagers later showed resentment at the suggestion that they should somehow raise attendance at the school. One man remarked, 'A person does not bear children like a dog—a litter of six or eight which all grow up at once! We can't bear children like dogs and send

---

[1] Subsequently the nomenclature was altered. Instead of reckoning in terms of two primary grades and four 'standards' of primary schooling, the system now runs from 'Standard I' to 'Standard VI'. I use the terms operative in 1964.

them all to school in the same year!' The District Commissioner must have forgotten the small size of the village, for most children did in fact attend school in Kuli or Nojane. (On the other hand, he might reasonably have complained that their attendance could be more regular, for some parents were in the habit of keeping children from school when there was urgent work to be done.)

They agreed, however, that they should raise the levy suggested by the District Commissioner. They appreciated also that any complaints of the new head-teacher—about the condition of the teachers' quarters, unpunctuality of children, delays in paying school-fees, etc.—should be dealt with for fear that they come to the ears of the District Commissioner and shake his faith in the villagers' hunger for educational facilities. In the following months the head-teacher raised various issues, and he always received a good hearing. The *lekgota* ordered measures to meet his demands, and if these were not always carried out, it was because of the difficulty of organising communal work-parties—a subject to which I shall return.

The main issue with which the *lekgota* was faced, however, was the levy. At first the villagers seemed to expect the District Commissioner to rule on the size of individual contributions. When it became evident that he would not, a meeting was held to consider the question.

The chief counsellor told the *lekgota*, 'The District Commissioner said he wants R200—"you must collect it and send it to me. If you can do that, I am sure that Government will help you build the school" (he said)'. The headman reproached the people:

I wonder why none of you has brought me money. Government has said that you must help yourselves. Everywhere except in Kuli, there are up-to-date school buildings. A European [a Government welfare officer on a tour] asked me where the money was. Everyone should sell a beast and bring money.

The headman's son followed up this last suggestion. He remarked that while the trader's prices for cattle were unsatisfactory, a cattle-market was being held shortly at Ghanzi, and they could realise good prices there. 'Let us all drive cattle to Ghanzi. Let us try, for this word of the District Commissioner about building the school is not a game. I am sorry, for Kuli is behind in everything.'

Somebody pointed out that this still left unanswered the question of how much each man should pay. The headman said, 'I want to answer this. You may pay more. You know you are working for the tribe.

However much you have, say R10, just give it to me. There are many works, not just one work, that we do.' He then suggested that 'each man must give R4 or R8 or R10. I mean a rich man. Men with two cattle can pay R1 only. This is possible.' Neither his son Matlopelwe, nor his grandson, the court-scribe, would accept this differential assessment. As the court-scribe said, 'The headman has eaten and now he is satisfied, for he is rich. We also want to be rich. Every man should give the same amount.' He reminded his grandfather that when the village had raised money for a borehole, the headman had made a disproportionate contribution, and that the other people had still been dissatisfied. 'Every man here should pay the same,' he concluded, 'for, rich or poor, your children attend school.' The headman retracted and agreed with him.

A citizen said that this was all very well, but he was too poor to raise more than about R1. Waatotsi attacked him scathingly. Everyone had agreed on the goal, but 'now people here say, I am not rich—and therefore there is no progress'. The citizen protested that he was just asking if he should bring only R1 if this was all he could raise. Waatotsi answered, 'if someone brings R1, I'll bring the same', and the headman's son reminded the citizen that he could hardly claim to be poor.

It was finally agreed that if the sum was to be raised, every citizen would have to contribute R4. A popular counsellor then called on all tax-payers to pay the subscription. He would record all payments. If the total raised was insufficient, a further levy would be set. The headman concurred: 'As we are here in the *kgota*, I will pay R4. That will be my notice. If the total is short we can increase the levy.' The popular counsellor then said, 'If people send cattle to the market and do not pay their subscriptions on their return, they should be brought to trial for despising the counsellors'.

The matter rested there until after the cattle-sale had been held at Ghanzi in July. At the following meeting of the *lekgota*, the headman announced that he wanted subscriptions from men of the age-set of Konothye (aged about thirty) and upwards, and that he wanted R4 from each man, rich or poor. He told the meeting: 'I do not want to talk to the District Commissioner about this. I just want him to be happy with the money we will subscribe.' Answering some complaints, the headman reminded the citizens of the arrangement to sell cattle at the Ghanzi sale to raise cash; those who had failed to do so could sell cattle to the trader. Mabote, the leader of the opposition Pebana faction, supported the headman, and a popular counsellor said: 'The headman tells the truth ... People have not subscribed, and some have not attended the *lekgota* meetings. Everyone should come and listen for himself. The money is for the tribe—the headman works for the tribe ... The District Commissioner wants money for the school.' The headman's son made a speech along similar lines.

Some contributions were paid in during the weeks and months that followed, and from time to time citizens were urged to pay at *lekgota* meetings. I attended one session at which two citizens came forward and paid R2 each, and a popular counsellor paid R4. The following debate ensued:

Waatotsi: If R2 is paid that means that there are two headmen in Kuli. You should pay R4 each. If you pay R2 you should promise to pay another R2 soon.

Headman Ramoŝwane: Bangologa, nobody should be forced. If you pay just R2 each, I will take you to the District Commissioner and say that the tribe despises the headman.

Moloise: I stand to say I cannot pay. One who pays only R2 is trying to make people force him. It is the same with one who pays nothing—he despises the headman. One who pays R2 must be told to bring the balance tomorrow. One who has not paid must pay.

Lebiki (one of the men who had paid in only R2): If a person pays R2, it may be that he has no more. Welcome it and tell him to go and look for the rest. If a man is rich, he is rich for himself, not for someone else. Some are rich, others are poor. We should not say a person despises the headman. He may just have no money. Nobody despises the law ...

Headman Ramoŝwane: You are wrong. If a man pays R2, he must bring another R2 tomorrow. We want money, even from the poor.

And then, towards the end of the year, came the news that the District Commissioner was being transferred. He was about to make a final tour of the villages. Two emergency *lekgota* sessions were called immediately before his arrival so that everything would be in order when he came. One of the key issues discussed was the state of the levy. Someone suggested that they put the matter before the next District Commissioner, but the headman said that the issue was the responsibility of the present official. Another man—a popular counsellor—complained that the headman demanded the money only when the District Commissioner was due, but this was refuted by the chief counsellor, who said that the only problem was that some people did not attend meetings regularly, and so did not know what had been decided. Mabote, the opposition leader, supported him, but appealed for consideration to be taken of the fact that some citizens had not been present when it was decided to sell cattle at the Ghanzi sale, and so could not be said to have committed themselves to this.[1]

A letter from the District Commissioner was then read by the court-scribe. The District Commissioner wrote that the Kuli school was to be upgraded by one standard, and perhaps even more if the enrolment increased and new buildings were erected. This moved some citizens to make excuses for not having paid, and several defaulters were called on by name to pay.

When the District Commissioner arrived and addressed the *lekgota* it was quickly evident to me (though perhaps not to the citizens) that he had allowed the arrangement with the villagers about the levy to slip his mind. (He had not mentioned the topic in the village for several months, but the villagers had thought that he was simply waiting in silence to see whether they would raise the money.) He told the *lekgota* that the Education Department had agreed to upgrade the school, but felt that the people of Kuli were not showing enough interest. A good way of demonstrating their eagerness for further educational facilities was to increase enrolment in the school and to raise a levy for new buildings. They would now need a new classroom, and should raise money for this.

A popular counsellor thanked the District Commissioner, and told him that the villagers had already raised R60 towards a new classroom. The District Commissioner replied that this was gratifying, and suggested R150 as a goal—was this reasonable? The popular counsellor thought it was. In fact, he said, the villagers were very satisfied, since the District Commissioner had originally asked for R200.

Summary

The demand for the expansion of the school was first pressed on the District Commissioner by the Kuli *lekgota*. He had money available for school building, and the Department of Education was willing to consider upgrading the school. He agreed therefore, but on condition that the villagers made a contribution.

For their part, the villagers were united. Everyone wanted the school to be upgraded. Even Mabote, the headman's leading opponent, supported the village goverment. The only contentious point was

---

[1] It should be noted that even if the *lekgota* decides on a measure, an absentee, or a person who abstains, may claim that he did not commit himself to it.

whether the levy should be uniformly or differentially assessed, but a common rate was quickly agreed upon. Once this point was settled, the village authorities exerted steady moral pressure on the citizens to pay their shares. The necessity for a common front was stressed frequently, but while speakers regularly referred to the fact that the District Commissioner and other Europeans were watching to see what their response would be, there was no support for the occasional recommendation that the District Commissioner should be given the names of those who did not pay.

Despite some success in raising the levy the project almost foundered, for two reasons. One was the poor communication with the District Commissioner. He neglected the project for many months, and forgot the original measures he had urged on the villagers. Moreover, his transfer at the crucial moment when the levy was well on the way to being raised jeopardised the whole policy. (It was only in 1967, under different circumstances, that the new classrooms at last materialised.)

The second reason was the difficulty the headman had in organising labour for communal projects. This meant that the teachers' repeated requests for improvements in their quarters and in the school facilities were not met; and this in turn raised the danger that the Education Department would decide that the villagers were not seriously committed to their school. When the building materials were finally delivered, they were allowed to deteriorate in the open for some time before work-parties could be organised. This problem—the problem of community labour—is distinct from the specific issue of school expansion, but I shall examine it here since it sheds light on the difficulty of administering policies, even when they are initiated by Government and supported by the villagers.

Community labour

The basic problem, solved only when the *Ipelegeng* programme was begun at the time of Independence, was that no material rewards were offered for labour on community projects. Young men, no longer organised in age-groups, and oriented towards a cash market for labour, were not prepared to cooperate. Women were generally kept at home to maintain domestic food supplies, though they were occasionally released for brief, pressing, and essentially female jobs, such as re-thatching the teachers' quarters, or preparing a hut for the District evangelist.

At one *lekgota* meeting, Waatotsi summed up pithily, if optimistically, the limited options:

The work is heavy in Kuli because we look for food. We must work and fine absentees and buy food with that money. The headman cannot help us with food . . . Even if we are old . . . we must try. When my children see me falling under my load, they will come and help. The children will never do it alone. We must go and oversee the work.

However, there was little support for fining absentees—this had been tried in the past, but failed. Nor were the young men moved by the labours of the old. It was commonplace at the time to see three or four elderly men shifting the building materials, without assistance.

This problem was later solved, at least temporarily, by the initiation of the Government *Ipelegeng* ('Food for Work') programme, but it remains a major stumbling block in the way of community development. Not only the school and the teachers' quarters, but even the borehole in Kuli deteriorated because the villagers were unable to organise efficient labour forces without outside assistance.

IV

I have been dealing with issues on which the villagers were united, if often impotent or poorly organised. But there are many issues which split the members of the *lekgota* into factions. As I said earlier, this is particularly likely when the ultimate decision is in the hands of the villagers and jobs or the internal power balance are at stake. Two issues of this kind were significant in Kuli affairs in 1964. One centred on the administration of the borehole. The other concerned the lack of participation in public affairs of certain sections of the village, and led the headman to overreach himself.

The borehole and the pumpers

Kuli has one borehole, which was sunk by the Public Works Department. The villagers are responsible for appointing and paying someone to operate and maintain it. This official is called the 'pumper'. Matlopelwe, the headman's son, held this position for a number of years. He was displaced in the course of a political crisis, in which Mabote's faction and the Silebe, together with the head-teacher, rounded on the headman. His successor, Morimomongwe, a popular counsellor, was a member of Mabote's faction.

In 1963 Morimomongwe left Kuli with a view to settling in Makunda. Before he left, he and Mabote installed his son Sekoma as pumper. This appointment was not ratified by the *lekgota* or the headman. Morimomongwe wrote to the *lekgota* from Makunda to say that his son Sekoma had succeeded him as pumper and should be paid his wages. The *lekgota* refused to consider the matter until Morimomongwe appeared before it in person. In mid-1964 Morimomongwe returned to Kuli, and Sekoma precipitated a crisis by going on strike and hiding the crank with which the borehole engine was started.

The *lekgota* then met to consider the situation. Two points were raised at once: by what right had Sekoma been made pumper? and should a new pumper be appointed? The headman demanded the immediate appointment of a new man. He told the *lekgota*:

The District Commissioner wants us to find another man for the engine. [This was, I think, untrue. The District Commissioner was probably unaware of the crisis.] Sekoma is like Morimomongwe—he now says that he will leave the engine. He did not come and tell me first. I am not against Morimomongwe and Sekoma. I tell you, Pebana men, you must look for a new pumper. I want a new pumper. I have no news and no case.

The two candidates for the post were Sekoma and a young man named Merahe. Merahe was an associate of the family-group of Haudwelwe, an ally of headman Ramošwane. Thus both of the Pebana factions had a candidate. The third political grouping, the Silebe, were uncommitted. Their choice was vital.

A Silebe popular counsellor called on the men in the *lekgota* to express their views. The decision should not be left to the counsellors. The headman's son, Matlopelwe, suggested a decision by a show of hands (something suggested from time to time, but seldom if ever resorted to). The Silebe counsellor then said that he was angry at the undisciplined behaviour of Tsenene's children (Morimomongwe and his son Sekoma). He would support Merahe, since a pumper should live near the borehole. The ultimate rationale was not compelling—both candidates lived near the borehole—but it softened the blow for Mabote's faction.

The headman, now secure of Silebe support, said that Mabote and Tsenene had acted wrongly in appointing a pumper without first getting his approval. He wanted to tell Mabote this. Mabote was absent. He had sent word that he was ill, but 'He is not sick, he is just against me'.

The discussion moved on to the salary which should be paid the pumper—it seemed that Merahe's appointment had been accepted.

Speakers agreed that all users of the borehole should contribute to the salary. The pumper should name his fee—'A Boer (an Afrikaans farmer) hiring a worker says what he will pay, and the worker can then complain. Tell him to name his salary.' It was also pointed out that the Ngologa do not count months as the Europeans do, and the pumper should expect his wages to be somewhat irregular.

But there were nevertheless signs of dissension below the surface, phrased in terms of a hesitation to accept personal responsibility for the decision. Morimomongwe himself said:

I ask the *lekgota* not to be angry. These men are afraid to say yes. When the headman asks whether we agree, we men in the *kgota* do not reflect that if one says yes one may affect years of another man's life. We want the headman to appoint, and we will agree. Do not point to one man and say, You are the one who said yes.

And another man said, 'I am speaking because men in the *kgota* will say that they were speaking and I just kept quiet. When, tomorrow, something goes wrong with the engine, men will say—*I* did not choose Merahe.'

Merahe duly took up the job of pumper, but after working for some months he went on strike and threatened to tell the District Commissioner that he had not received his wages. The *lekgota* met to investigate. It soon became evident—as Waatotsi remarked—that Merahe had not yet been paid because the supporters of Sekoma (Mabote's faction) were dissatisfied with the appointment and were withholding their contributions to his salary.

The issue of Sekoma's dismissal without payment was raised again.

Mabote: If a man dies his son inherits. Thus Sekoma took over from Morimomongwe.

Waatotsi: The headman refused to pay Sekoma because he was put in by the former pumper. Sekoma can ask for money from Morimomongwe! The headman refused to pay Sekoma because later Morimomongwe would return and demand his money.

Citizen: The headman was right. Morimomongwe ought to pay since he employed Sekoma.

Despite the continued opposition of Mabote and his faction, it was clear from the debate that opinion had hardened for the headman. The argument was cut short by the arrival of the District Commissioner, who immediately began his own session of the *lekgota*. When he had completed his business, the headman asked him to hear 'the case of the pumper': Merahe, the pumper, had not been paid for his services by some of the villagers who used the borehole. Presented with the issue in these terms, the District Commissioner naturally endorsed Merahe's right to payment, and he instructed the court-scribe to see that he was paid, and that anyone who failed to contribute was banned from using the borehole.

This temporary resolution was effected in August 1964. It was not long, however, before new crises occurred. In November, a serious dispute about the purchase of diesel fuel for the borehole engine came to a head. The users of the borehole were organised into two groups, each of which was supposed to buy the supplies of fuel in turn. These groups corresponded closely to the two Pebana factions. One included Ramoŝwane, Riphoni, Haudwelwe and Monantwe; the other included Mabote, Tsenene, Morimomongwe, Salakae and an independent, Mahupunyane. At a meeting of the *lekgota*, headman Ramoŝwane's son Matlopelwe charged that Mabote's group had not contributed its share of the fuel. He had been forced to sell an ox of Ramoŝwane's in order to buy a drum of diesel fuel himself. This contention was not disputed, and Tsenene agreed that his group should make its contribution. However, the problem came before the *lekgota* once again in December, and it had still not been settled when I left the country at the end of the year.

On my return to Kuli in 1966, I found that the arrangements for the administration of the borehole had degenerated into near-chaos. A number of small groups had bought their own belts for the engine and small supplies of fuel, and were operating the borehole for themselves whenever necessary. There was no unified management, and the condition of the borehole was deteriorating. It was often used unoiled, and it frequently broke down.

In October 1966, a new crisis was precipitated: Mabote's son hid the crank with which the borehole was started. This forced a fresh confrontation of the two Pebana factions. The District Councillor was now on the scene, however, and he conducted an enquiry into the problem at a meeting of the *lekgota*. The debate revealed the extent to which the conflict had escalated.

Headman Ramoŝwane's son Matlopelwe made the first statement:

I do not know the master of the borehole in this country. At first, diesel and oil were brought by the tribe. Now everyone buys for himself. Secondly, belts: everyone now has his own belt [a detachable and perishable part of the machinery]. The tribe has a belt, but I bought one because there is misunderstanding among us. The engine pumps without oil.

After ascertaining that the District Councillor was enquiring on his own account and not for Government, another citizen, who did not himself use the borehole, said:

The only problem is oil. Many people do not water at the borehole [they use wells in the pan instead]. Some remain. We shall fight. We do not know who is responsible. One said, I bought oil; another said, I bought diesel fuel; another said, we all bought. I travel about a lot and so I don't know whether Mabote or the headman is responsible.

Morimomongwe then challenged some remarks of Matlopelwe, and the *kgota* echoed with factional accusations and counter-accusations. Matlopelwe, for example, said that when he had replaced the borehole belt he had laid out over R14—but 'that side' (pointing to the north of the village, where Mabote and his allies live) only contributed R4. Mabote countered that they were dissatisfied with the attempts of the headman's son to control them. 'Matlopelwe is responsible for these problems,' he said. 'He does not report to his father but argues with his father's brothers.'

After some heated argument, a junior member of Mabote's faction, Lebiki, said: 'These things are bad because there is no pumper. We want a man who can pump our engine but who comes from another village. I say what I think.' This proposal to resolve the dispute by taking it out of the village arena and involving an uncommitted outsider was later implemented, in slightly different fashion, by the District Councillor. I shall deal with his intervention later.

Summary

The conflicts had roots in earlier confrontations between the factions of Mabote and the headman. The headman's son, who had been the first pumper, had lost the position to Morimomongwe of Mabote's faction. The conflicts I witnessed, which saw the position pass to a man in the headman's faction once more (though one not related to the headman), and finally resulted in the development of an anarchic situation, can be divided into three rounds.

The first round began when Morimomongwe left Kuli and his son, Sekoma, took over his job as pumper without the consent of the headman or *lekgota*. A crisis was precipitated when Morimomongwe returned to Kuli and Sekoma went on strike, putting the borehole out of action, and demanded his wages. The headman, with the support of the Silebe, ignored Sekoma's demands and installed his own candidate as pumper.

The headman's victory was not decisive. Several citizens indicated that they were withholding public approval of the appointment, and were therefore not committed to recognising the pumper. Round two followed swiftly. Mabote and his supporters withheld their contributions to Merahe's wages, and Merahe went on strike and hid the crank to the borehole. When the issue came before the *lekgota*, the Silebe and several influential neutrals supported the headman. Mabote's attempt to raise Sekoma's case once more was defeated. The headman then clinched his (temporary) victory by manoeuvring the District Commissioner into recognising Merahe as the official pumper, and ordering that all users of the borehole should contribute towards his wages.

Far from resolving the matter, this crisis led to an extension of the area of conflict. All cooperation, even on the purchase of fuel, ceased. Small groups operated the borehole for themselves, and when the headman's family-group was suspected of asserting a special right to the use of the borehole, Mabote's son detonated the third crisis by hiding the crank once more. This time the District Councillor intervened, and a possible resolution was attempted through the transfer of control over the borehole to external authorities.

The headman and the counsellor

This case directly concerned the exercise of authority. A popular counsellor from the Silebe group had been instructed by the headman to handle the preliminaries of an assault case in which two Silebe youths were accused. The accused decamped, and the headman held the counsellor responsible. Moreover, he suspected the counsellor of not pressing the Silebe to attend sessions of the *lekgota*. Attendance was low, and absenteeism meant inefficient decision-making, for men may feel committed to follow the ruling of the *lekgota* only if they participated in its deliberations and made their support public. Absenteeism may also be a sign of opposition to the headman.

The headman decided to take action against the counsellor, and at a meeting of the *lekgota* he and his chief counsellor required a fine from Mokgethi (the counsellor in question). Mokgethi demanded to know what the fine was for. The chief counsellor told him, 'I want a fine because for two months the headman has called meetings of the *lekgota* and none of your people have come ... At least tell the *lekgota*, I informed so-an-so, but he hasn't turned up.' It was evident from the subsequent debate, however, that it was the double dereliction of duty that was being held against Mokgethi: the disappearance of the Silebe youths wanted for assault was the last straw.

Mokgethi countered in various ways. He said he was ill. He raised procedural objections—fines should be demanded immediately a *lekgota* session began, not, as in this case, half-way through, after other matters had been raised. He also claimed that he had not been duly warned that a fine would be demanded of him at the meeting. Finally, he obliquely attacked the headman, and indicated that his rights as a counsellor to know the business of the session beforehand had been ignored.

The headman would have none of this. He said:

Riphoni [the chief counsellor] is right. He speaks my word. He is the man I asked to summon a *lekgota*, but people did not come for they do not listen to me. He is my big counsellor. I have chosen him as my big counsellor. You are small counsellors. You can't argue with him. He is right.

Mokgethi answered:

I understand. I agree with my superior counsellor. The headman and his brother agree, and I am lost. I have been far away. These are new words to me. It is now for the *lekgota*, and I will speak after them. I have already said I am ill.

The argument was then taken up by Modjathoši, the other Silebe popular counsellor, and he raised substantive constitutional issues. He pointed out that it had been agreed in the past that men who failed to attend *lekgota* meetings without good reason should be liable to a fine. But the headman was proposing something new—to fine counsellors if citizens from their part of the village did not attend meetings. He said:

Now this fine of Riphoni, we do not know what this law is. A law should be made in the *kgota* so that even those working in the bush may know. We hear the headman and his son making a new law. Even a white man does not make a law if his labourers are not present. It is a law, not one hand [i.e. the headman cannot pass a law without the approval of the *lekgota*].

The headman appeared to be unmoved, but shortly after Modjathoši's speech the matter was dropped and the *lekgota* proceeded to discuss the assault case which had been one of the causes of the headman's displeasure.

On the following day the *lekgota* reassembled, and on this occasion Mabote, the headman's leading opponent, was present. Modjathoši asked permission to summarise the issue for Mabote's benefit, which he proceeded to do in the following terms. Riphoni had demanded a fine, but the counsellors had said that this could not be done until notice of the law had been given to the tribe in the *kgota*. Riphoni had answered that he was only fining Mokgethi, but the people said that a law must apply to all, and could not just be made and applied to one man. The counsellors had agreed. The law was now to be debated again.

The headman and his chief counsellor maintained their position of the previous day, but one of the headman's allies, Haudwelwe, warned him: 'It is a bad thing. People will not agree. Tomorrow it will be a trap to catch you. You are angry and therefore do not understand us even if we speak the truth.'

Modjathoši then made another speech. He rehearsed the various essays in legislation which the *lekgota* had attempted in the past. Laws had been passed setting fines for non-attendance at *lekgota* meetings; laying down the wages which should be paid for communal labour; and providing for fines for those who failed to participate in such work. He said that the headman had passed these laws with the *lekgota*, but had later failed to enforce them. He wanted the headman to make this law and to enforce it—but he should drop his demand for a fine now.

The headman rejected this face-saving formula. A visitor from Kalkfontein now intervened. He made a lengthy speech, dealing mainly in large generalities about the ideal roles of headmen, citizens, counsellors and *lekgota*. He then said that he would judge the case himself. There was some applause. He said the headman should retire to his home in seemly fashion and leave the *lekgota* to settle the matter.

Although Mabote had not openly committed himself, Modjathoši treated him as an ally, and it was clear that the general feeling was against the headman. The headman was supported only by the chief counsellor and the court-scribe, his grandson. The *lekgota* passed on to other topics, and neither the proposed law nor the demand for a fine from Mokgethi were mentioned again.

Summary

When the conflict about the pumper was at its peak, the headman steam-rollered Mabote's faction with the support of the Silebe. In this case, pitted against the Silebe, the headman could not even command the sure loyalty of some of his closest allies, and Mabote, while not intervening actively, indicated his sympathy for the Silebe counsellors. Eventually, the intervention of an outsider allowed the headman to retreat with some dignity, but there was no disguising his defeat. He had attempted to assert an authoritarian control over his popular counsellors and failed. The weakness of his constitutional position— so skilfully exposed by Modjathoši—was crucial to his failure, but this case illustrates once again that two factions defeat one.

v

Thus in the years immediately preceding Botswana's Independence, policy-making and administration in the village was riddled with problems. Often the villagers had little or no say in determining policy, and when the decisions were their responsibility, it was sometimes impossible to reach the point of action. There were three main reasons for this state of affairs. First, communication between the village and the District Commissioner was poor. The villagers had little chance of bringing their views to the attention of Government, and on his side the District Commissioner was often out of touch. Continuity, too, was lacking. Secondly, where decisions were left to the villagers, it might be impossible to find a line of action which commanded general support, and hence decisions were often unenforceable. There was little chance of compelling a dissident minority to submit to a majority decision. Thirdly, the executive arm of the *lekgota*, the village government, was weak and sometimes internally divided. Nobody was eager to assert authority, or very effective if they attempted to do so.

The picture changed between 1965 and 1967. First, the new government under Sir Seretse Khama was prepared to take new administrative initiatives where the colonial government had shown itself unwilling to act. Secondly, an international famine-relief programme allowed the Botswana Government to mount its *Ipelegeng* project, handing out food in return for labour on community development tasks. Thirdly, and most important at the village level, the establishment of District Councils in 1966 provided new communication links between village and District, and brought into political prominence the District's 'new men', who provided a novel force within the village political system. The District Councillor is often detached from village factions—in Kuli he is an outsider—and with his position at District headquarters he is able to win support from villagers for new policies and to exert authority within the village political system.

The impact of these developments was immediately apparent when I returned to Kuli in 1966–7. The question of the Kuli school had been raised at the very first meeting of the District Council, and although it was referred to the Ministry of Education this was a swift sign that the villagers were now in a position to press some initiatives on the District authorities. Similarly, a dispute with the Herero of Makunda over grazing privileges was debated by the District Council, although the Kuli authorities had repeatedly failed to interest the District Commissioner in the matter.

It appeared further that some District Councillors wanted to take some policy matters out of the village arena. Their aim was to transfer to the District Council's authority what the village authorities could not manage. Kuli's borehole troubles—duplicated in several villages—provided the first target. Jankie and the Kuli District Commissioner proposed that the District Council should administer village boreholes sunk by Government. It would assess watering fees on the basis of individual stock holdings, supervise the collection of fees, and pay the pumpers.

The District Councillors were also influential within the *lekgota*, often guiding policy-decisions. The Kuli District Councillor (and some in other villages) actually presided over regular sessions of the *lekgota*, and it was only in judicial hearings that the headman retained the unchallenged direction of meetings. The extent to which the District Councillor actually dominated sessions varied from village to village, and within villages according to his own personal ability and the prevailing power balance. But although he was everywhere influential, he was seldom allowed to dictate. In Kuli the District Councillor was on one occasion prevented by the *lekgota* from even discussing details of a building programme, because several counsellors and influential elders were absent.

To illustrate the impact of the District Councillor in the *lekgota*, I present a description of how a series of decisions were reached in the Kuli *lekgota* under his leadership. These decisions were made at one meeting, held in October 1966, and the process can be contrasted with the examples I have given of decision-making in Kuli in 1964. The issue was how the building project on which the villagers were engaged—the construction of a classroom and a storage-hut for school-feeding—should be prosecuted.[1]

Luther Sakgu, the District Councillor, summoned the meeting, and

---

[1] The organisation of communal labour was facilitated at this time by Government's *Ipelegeng* programme. *Ipelegeng* (literally, 'life yourselves up'—a BDP slogan), was rendered into English as 'Food for Work', and was instituted in order to promote community development projects at the same time as providing famine relief.

about sixteen men and eight women attended. The women sat in a group outside the *kgota* fence. Luther opened the meeting with a prayer, and then instructed the citizens on the way in which he wished the debate to be conducted. He wanted to hear the views of at least four men on any points which might arise, and then see by a show of hands how many agreed or disagreed. If some people were 'as one man', for example brothers, only one need speak. Everyone present should contribute his views.

He then raised the main topic, the building programme. Only two or three men were assisting the large group of women who were doing the building. Should the work be left to the women? Matlopelwe, the headman's son, said that men should help: no house can be built by women alone. Lebiki agreed, and so did visitors from Nojane and Hukuntsi, who said that in their villages men were assisting the women. Luther then remarked that everyone was agreed, and said that on Monday all the men should attend and bring tools and materials for building a frame for the roof.

Luther then raised a second problem—a supervisor should be appointed. He said, 'I am a messenger. I make my speech and go home. If I am not here there is no progress. I live in Nojane, not here, and when I come it is just to see whether there is progress. Therefore you must choose a supervisor.' The headman agreed that a local man should supervise the work, and asked whether Mabote, Morimomongwe and the Silebe leaders were participating. This was in the nature of a rhetorical question: he was fully aware that they were not. The chief counsellor submitted that the Silebe and the young men were withholding their labour, so raising a further problem, which Luther immediately seized upon—'What must we do if your children do not come?' he asked. 'I ask the *lekgota*, not the headman, for it is the headman who judges them.' A visitor from Hukuntsi and Mabote spoke on this point, stressing that the young men should work. Luther said that two men had now answered, and that he wanted the views of two others. Two other men duly had their say.

Luther then returned to the main point at issue. Two people, one man and one woman, should be chosen to supervise the work. In answer to questions he said that this was the arrangement in Nojane, Hukuntsi and elsewhere. It emerged in discussion that Mabote's younger brother, Mokgetise, had been chosen for the job, but he was not present at the meeting. Mabote remarked that the Silebe popular counsellors were also absent, and said, 'We cannot choose a man who is absent. It is hard because the counsellors are not here.' The headman's son, Matlopelwe, agreed, and called on the only popular counsellor present, Morimomongwe, to guide the discussion.

Morimomongwe argued that a man without much property to look after should be chosen, because he would not be distracted by the needs of his cattle. He nominated Mokgetise, who, as I have said, had been previously appointed. Luther asked those in favour to raise their hands, but nobody stirred. Some people suggested that Mokgetise might prove unreliable—after all, he had not attended the *lekgota*—but it was pointed out that he had successfully supervised a previous job. Morimomongwe put his name forward once more, and this time some people indicated their support. Luther then said, 'I agree that Mokgetise should be at the head.'

This settled, Luther raised the next problem. He wanted the *lekgota* to choose a woman who would be able to keep a register of people who participated in the work, so that they could later be rewarded appropriately with *Ipelegeng* food. Morimomongwe and others urged that the permission of the girl's father should be sought first; and that in general women should work only with the permission of their fathers or husbands. Luther agreed with him, but when Morimomongwe went on rather irrelevantly to lament Government's demand for new buildings, he pulled him up sharply. Luther pointed out the advances which had been made in other villages, and admonished Morimomongwe to be a true counsellor and encourage people to work.

From time to time during the debate speakers had returned to the problem of the young men who would not work. Morimomongwe now pointed out that they did not even attend *lekgota* meetings, and suggested that they be forced to do so. Luther agreed, and brought the debate to an end by setting the date for the commencement of the next stage in the building, and confirming Mokgetise's appointment. He then led the *lekgota* on to other topics.

In contrasting this debate to earlier ones I have described, the outstanding feature is the strong chairmanship. Luther even attempted to introduce 'Western' committee techniques, and if he was unsuccessful in this he nevertheless controlled the course of the debate effectively. He did not force the *lekgota* to accept particular proposals of his own: his achievement was rather to ensure that effective decisions were made. This may be an indication that he recognised the limits of his authority, and certainly the *lekgota* asserted itself when it insisted on a partial lead from a popular counsellor.

The issues did not raise factional feelings. The supervisory job was unpaid, and several speakers agreed that it should be given to a man without distracting responsibilities. Mokgetise, a property-less popular counsellor who had once before successfully supervised a building job, and who had some skill in construction, was an obvious choice. When Luther was faced with a factional conflict, over the borehole, he asked for all points of view and then attempted to take the matter out of the villagers' control and hand over responsibility to the District Council. Perhaps this will set a pattern for similar situations in the future. In any case, it indicated the resources at his command for the handling of such conflicts.

Luther's success in organising communal labour should be noted. This was due in part, of course, to Government's food-for-work, but he (and District Councillors in other villages) showed considerable initiative and energy, and proved that in certain areas the District Councillor can now provide strong executive leadership.

I have mentioned that District Councillors sometimes attempted to commit the villagers to new initiatives. The District Councillor in Nojane, with his pressure-group, was particularly successful, and he lent his support to Luther for similar initiatives in Kuli. The establishment of a Nojane-Kuli cooperative was the most novel plan, and Jankie of Nojane mobilised a major educational campaign, even bringing the MP of Northern Kgalagadi District (who had started a cooperative in Matšeng) to press the project. As Jankie saw it, the problem was simply to make the old men understand. With his influence and political talent he seemed well on the way to success when I left the District in 1967.

VI

I have been dealing with external and internal policy-making. In the following chapter, I turn to the decision-making process in judicial matters, which presents a sharp contrast to internal policy-making. The conflicts, improvisations and manoeuvres of internal policy-making seem on the surface totally unrelated to the ordered, traditional mechanism of the legal case, where fixed procedures, precedents and shared interests combine to smooth the way to an accepted decision. Moving from one to the other, the *lekgota* seems to be transformed; but, of course, it remains the same body, and its transformations illuminate its basic structure.

8

THE JUDICIAL PROCESS AND THE
ADMINISTRATION OF THE LAW

I

The *lekgota* is a statutory court, a part of the national judicial structure;[1] and many of the issues with which it deals may also fall within the province of the police. Nevertheless, the national system of law-enforcement is only a limiting factor in its operations. Official supervision of the *lekgota* as a court is minimal. The District Commissioner occasionally checks the court-records, but rarely challenges any judgment (and the court-record provides little basis for serious review, since it usually provides few details). Appeals are infrequent, and they are discouraged. Official policy is to refer as many matters as possible to the *lekgota*. The headman and the citizens also prefer to settle disputes within the village.

Consequently the most immediate influences on the administration of the law are local. The principles applied by the *lekgota* derive mainly from the structure of jural relationships within the village—the villagers are concerned to prevent outside intervention; once this is secured, home-grown legal principles are applied. (This is, of course, satisfactory to a Government which accepts the value of 'customary law' and is, in any case, desperately short of administrative staff.)[2]

But while the judicial process is concerned with intra-village social relationships, and active external intervention is of restricted scope, legal issues, unlike issues of internal policy, do not split the *lekgota* into factions. This is due in large part to the jural structure of the

[1] These courts are designated as Headmen's Courts with powers scheduled as D (Civil) and H (Criminal). That is: 'They have in practically every case civil powers up to a subject-matter valued at R50, ten bovines or fifty small stock, and criminal powers up to a sentence of imprisonment for three months, a fine of R20, or five bovines or twenty small stock, and whipping up to four strokes.' (Hailey, 1953: 227.) Witchcraft and some other matters are excluded from their jurisdiction, and in colonial days they could not normally try Europeans. Finally, as Hailey remarks, even the higher customary courts were vested with the administration of the statutory law to only a minor degree (1953: 228).

[2] The Botswana Government is currently reviewing the operation of customary courts, and its policy may change, despite the practical difficulties in the way of reform of these courts.

family-group corporation. The *lekgota* treats it as a jural unit, and the group head is responsible for the torts of members and minors. Since the family-group is a property-owning group in which the rights of members are intertwined, it is in the interests of group members to prevent individual wrong-doing which may bring economic and moral loss to the group. Further, the group head's reputation with his peers suffers if he cannot control his members, and he is usually eager to collaborate with the community at large to see that a wrong is redressed. One might argue that this is a necessary investment for his own security —one's son is a defendant today, but tomorrow he may be an appellant, and so it is in one's interest in the long run to support the authority of the court. In any case, the observed fact is that citizens do not normally defend fellow members of family-groups unless the case against them is not clearly proved; and even put pressure on a guilty party to accept the judgment of the *lekgota*. The defendant is isolated, and, under pressure from his close agnates, has little choice but to submit to the judgment.

Other close kin play a secondary but important role in exerting moral pressure on a guilty party. It is noteworthy that in Kuli the most persistent law-breaker, whom I have heard dismissed with the ultimate condemnation, *ha se mothyo* (he is not a person), was without close kinship ties with other citizens, was the only adult male in his family-group, and lived on the outskirts of the village. The carelessness of young men may similarly be due in part to their relative independence of the family-group, because of their cash-earnings abroad, and their freedom from marital ties.[1]

This reliance on the moral unity of the family-group as against an individual transgressor—the court's ultimate dependence on agnatic authority—prevents the *lekgota* from acting effectively in a dispute within the family-group. Where such a dispute comes before the *lekgota* (which is rare) it is accepted unwillingly, and often marks a stage in the fission of the family-group concerned.

This delicate balance depends on an acceptance of the *lekgota*'s objectivity as a court, at least where citizens are embroiled in a dispute. The high moral valuation of the law and of legal processes is crucial.

[1] Thus Krige and Krige (following Malinowski) suggest that when the court's ruling is accepted the determining factor is 'the continuous pressure of institutionalised obligations, the impossibility of doing without tangible day-to-day mutualities, and the disorganisation caused by failure of the long-term reciprocities' (1943: 200). This comes from a discussion of the courts of another Sotho-speaking people, the Transvaal Lovedu.

Force is lacking (except in Hukuntsi, where the police are always being called in), and no one is in a position to bend the law.

These principles apply only where male citizens are involved in both sides of a case, and to their full extent only where Ngologa are involved, particularly men enmeshed in the network of kinship and affinity within the village. Women and Bushmen cannot exercise jural rights. Rights in them are exercised by male citizens in their capacity as husbands, fathers, brothers or masters, and only they should bring cases on behalf of these jural minors. Today, the police or District Commissioner may insist that the *lekgota* admit the complaint of a particular woman or a Bushman, but instead of ordering compensation, as is usual, the *lekgota* may impose a penal fine on the offender, the money going to the District Treasury. This brings out the special factor in these cases: Government is treated as the complainant.

Other minority elements, although accepted as citizens with all jural rights, may feel nevertheless that they are not given a fair deal by the *lekgota*. A Ngologa immigrant to Kalkfontein, for example, told me that 'here people follow their prejudices, and if you are not one of them you get no justice in the *kgota*'. The European trader in that village told me that he had stopped hauling thieves before the *lekgota* because 'they all gang up on you'. Similarly, the Kalkfontein Herero prefer to settle their disputes outside the *lekgota*. There are grounds for these feelings. The law being enforced may be foreign to a Herero or a Nama Hottentot, and the careful impartiality of the court as between citizens may be strained when a citizen is charged by an outsider. Further, the stranger is outside the web of multiplex relations, and therefore the continuity of fundamental relationships within the community is not at stake. On the other hand, this lessens the pressure on outsiders to comply with the law. Herero and Nama may be disciplined by their own groups, but the Bushmen often show no concern for the norms operating within the Ngologa political community.

II

These preliminary remarks are intended to clear the ground for a discussion of the various moots and courts within the village, of which the *lekgota* is the busiest and most important.

I have mentioned the fact that cases involving members of a family-group rarely go before the *lekgota*. These cases, and often marital disputes, are usually brought in the first instance before a kinship (or domestic) moot, the lowest-level dispute-settling body in the village. Such a moot can only arbitrate, and its range is effectively limited to disputes involving members, minors or associates of a family-group. The following case illustrates the procedure of the kinship moot, and its composition.

A kinship moot: the case of the Rakile wife

Leswape, the grandson of Headman Ramoŝwane and a member of his family-group, had not been married long. His wife had recently been through a confinement, and during this period Leswape had developed the habit of visiting other women in the village at night. One night he came home late and he and his wife had a quarrel, ostensibly about who should attend to the crying baby. Blows were exchanged.

The following morning Leswape went to report the quarrel to Haudwelwe, the head of a neighbouring family-group, who is his father's father's elder brother's son. Leswape's father was away at the time, and Haudwelwe took the matter to Ramoŝwane, in his capacity as head of Leswape's family-group. Ramoŝwane called for a discussion (*puo*), which took place that evening in the courtyard of Leswape's hut.

The meeting was attended by the older men and women of the family-group, and, in addition, Haudwelwe, and the mother and sisters of Leswape's wife, who were in the village to help look after the baby. (See Fig. 6.)

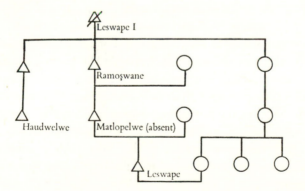

Fig. 6. The composition of a kinship moot.

Leswape spoke first. He described the quarrel, and concluded 'therefore I want the parent of my wife and my parents to give us the law (*molao*), for we are still young and know nothing about marriage'.

Haudwelwe said he was pleased with Leswape's speech. Leswape's wife was in error: she should care for Leswape and the baby and everything in the hut. Leswape, similarly, should care for his wife, baby and household goods, and everything would be peaceful. Ramoŝwane said he was the grandfather of Leswape and his wife. He was pleased that Leswape had reported this matter to Haudwelwe. Leswape was right to want peace in his home. Leswape's wife was foolish, for by their law she should take complaints against Leswape to Leswape's mother and to the family-group head, who would then call Leswape and ask him why he always fought with his wife.

Leswape's wife said that she understood, but she had a problem— and she broadened the discussion by introducing quarrels she and Leswape had about who controlled the household goods. Leswape argued that in Pebana custom the husband had complete control; and that his wife, who came from the Rakile clan, 'takes their laws'. The headman and his wife both supported Leswape, Ramoŝwane citing his own intervention on the husband's side when Leswape's parents had quarrelled over the same issue.

Broader issues of proper conduct and the background of this particular marriage were then introduced. Leswape's mother said, 'When Leswape's wife was confined, I wrote to her mother and she came here. When she came out of confinement she was given directions (*melao*) together with Leswape, instructing them not to fight. I don't want Leswape to fight in front of his mother-in-law.' And she warned that when the final bridewealth payment was due, the wife's family would demand a special fine for misconduct (*biŝana*).

Ramoŝwane referred to the background of the marriage, complaining that despite the close relationship between the parties, his family had not been fairly treated. His wife struck a more pacific note. She reminded the young couple that they were both Christians, and congratulated them on having referred their problem to the family for arbitration. In conclusion she returned to the point which Leswape's mother had made: 'you have seen that you made a mistake before your mother-in-law. You and your wife must know that this woman is your mother.'

I am concerned here only with the light this case throws on the kinship or domestic moot. First, the structure of authority is based on the family-group, but has certain peculiarities. Leswape took the matter in the first instance to a close agnate outside the group. This was the correct action, for one should not take one's problem to a man directly in authority over one. As an informant explained to me, 'If one approaches one's "father" directly, he will ask why one has not taken the matter to his "younger brother". This is because my "father" cannot swear at me, or use bitter words, while his "brother" can if necessary.'[1] Further, women were actively involved, although they are politico-jural minors and have no say in other dispute-settling groups.

Secondly, the norms invoked were of two kinds: general rules which apply to all husbands, wives, sons-in-law and daughters-in-law; and specific, perhaps unusual, familial customs. Leswape was told to modify his insistence on the latter in order to show respect for the general proprieties, while his wife was advised that the general norms implied submission to familial custom. Other moral and practical arguments were added to these, including appeals to Christian responsibilities, and to worldly experience—e.g. it is not wise to 'joke' too much with one's wife.

Finally, the moot did not limit itself to the immediate dispute. Nor did it impose penalties or formulate a specific solution to the problems of the marriage. The whole relationship was discussed, and the couple were urged by kin whom they should respect to mend their ways and behave properly.

Personnel, principles and procedures are determined by the fact that this moot falls within the domestic domain of social action. A closely integrated family-group alliance may also be the basis of a kinship moot which would operate in a similar fashion. Once a matter enters the public domain, however, everything changes—but intermediate between the two arenas is a marginal judicial institution, the sector moot.

At an early stage in my field-study, a Tswana schoolmaster in Kalkfontein remarked to me that a peculiarity of the local social organisation was that there was no formally constituted courts below the *lekgota*. Counsellors or sub-clan heads may accept complaints and carry out preliminary investigations, but they rarely arbitrate and hardly ever impose sentences of any kind. In contrast to the Tswana chiefs, Ngologa headmen do not encourage administrative subdivision (for one thing, their communities are much smaller), and they take seriously any challenge to the headman's right to judge all matters, except intra-family affairs. Nevertheless, a few cases are dealt with at a level intermediate to the family-group and the political community. I describe

---

[1] While not technically a 'father's younger brother', Haudwelwe was often treated as such by members of Ramošwane's family-group. Leswape might have approached Riphoni, but he was away at the time.

here a trial mounted in the sector moot of the Silebe (the only cohesive sub-clan in Kuli). It illustrates the procedures of the moot, its personnel, and its uneasy relationship to the headman.

The sector moot: a neighbourhood affair

The matter was heard in a clearing in the Silebe sector of Kuli. Masime presided, and the other Silebe elders, including the two counsellors were also present.[1] The parties, B and T, were not Silebe. They were the only representatives in Kuli of two minor clans, but both lived near the Silebe, and T (the complainant) was related to some of the Silebe elders and closely identified with the Silebe sub-clan.

B was accused of stealing a goat from T's kraal. The hide and a horn of the goat were produced in evidence, and a number of witnesses identified them as belonging to one of T's goats. After the parties and witnesses had been cross-examined, it was clear that B was guilty. The members of the moot ordered him to recompense T and warned that if he did not pay, the matter would be taken to the headman. B's own sons testified against him and urged him to pay, and in the opinion of some participants this 'shamed' him and persuaded him to submit to the moot's order.

The moot's procedures were very like those of the *lekgota*. The form of the trial, the sentence and the threat to invoke the headman's authority all oriented the proceedings towards the politico-jural domain (despite the fact that the structure of the moot was based on that of the Silebe sub-clan). But the political legitimacy of the moot was dubious. In the view of most citizens the constitutional duty of counsellors and sub-clan heads is to prepare a case for the *lekgota* rather than to try it. At the period when this trial took place, the Silebe were in many ways withholding support from the headman and *lekgota*,[2] and B himself had recently challenged the *lekgota*'s authority.

The headman saw the judicial activity of the Silebe moot as a challenge to his authority. 'They do not respect laws (*melao*),' he told me. 'They steal laws and make other *makgota*.' He argued that any judicial activity which substituted for his own court was a sign of insubordination—'it is like fighting with me'.

This tension between the dispute-settling authority of the village

[1] Masime had recently resigned the headship of the Silebe sub-clan to his father's older brother's son, Mothibakgomo, but since the latter was a young man he retained a guiding role in some situations.

[2] Cf. the case entitled the *Headman and the Counsellor*, described in the previous chapter.

headman and *lekgota* and the sector moots is less sharp in multi-tribal villages and in the isolated hamlets of large villages, for there headmen are prepared to tolerate greater independence. By and large, however, headmen jealously guard their judicial prerogatives. They have not only the duty but the right to settle disputes outside the circle of the family-group. Consequently, sector moots are not a prominent institution in Ngologa villages. They tend to be marginal judicial institutions with ambiguous legitimacy, ill-defined functions and vague principles of recruitment.

III

While the *lekgota* is the main village court, the village government may employ judicial committees to facilitate or supplement its work. Counsellors, usually working together with the headman (or at least in consultation with him) regularly carry out preliminary investigations before a matter comes before the *lekgota*. They weigh complaints, contact witnesses, even carry out searches or inspections. Occasionally a small group, normally led by the headman and including some counsellors and other citizens, will settle a case outside the *kgota*. This procedure may carry with it political risks, however, and it is employed mainly in cases involving outsiders, particularly Bushmen. Such a tribunal would be unlikely to impose penalties.

A preliminary investigation: the case of a hungry Bushman

The committee which met to investigate an allegation of stock-theft against a Bushman gathered under a tree near the headman's hut. It included the headman, the chief counsellor (who was the complainant) and his son, and three other citizens. The accused, a Lala Bushman, was accompanied by members of his family.

The accused admitted his guilt, but was unrepentant. He said, 'I would kill any goat I see . . . I was hungry'. He accepted that he should be brought before the *lekgota*, but refused to consider paying compensation. A citizen cross-examined him. 'Do you want to be lashed?' 'It does not matter.' 'Can we send you to prison?' 'No—I killed a goat, not a cow.' (Laughter, and he repeats his statement.) 'If I am lashed I will go back to South West Africa. I get food there.' 'If you won't go to prison, will you repay the loss of the goat?' 'You say you will lash me, so why should I?' The citizen pointed out to the complainant that he would get nothing if the accused was lashed, and he urged the accused to pay compensation.

The headman commented, 'This man does not mind confessing to his crime. He just wants to fight. That means he despises the *lekgota*. He does not know that the person who questions him is helping him.' The complainant's son asked what one should do to a cheeky criminal, and the headman told him that he should be brought before the *lekgota* so that he could be questioned by everyone ('even you!').

The facts of the case were also reviewed. The complainant's son related how he had followed the spoor of the lost goat and found the accused eating it in the company of some Lala children. Under cross-examination the accused and the children stated that he had stolen and killed the goat on his own. The children had joined him only when they smelt the meat being cooked.

The headman then established which of the Lala elders could be held responsible for the torts of the accused, and instructed one of them, despite his protests, that the *lekgota* would regard him as the 'father' of the accused. He agreed that the children were not accomplices, and that only the accused should be brought to trial. He concluded: 'We have just taken statements.[1] We must go before the full *lekgota*.'

The chief counsellor agreed. He said, 'The members of the *lekgota* are not present. We must wait for them. "Government" says Bushmen are his, but they just destroy our things. What can we do, since "Government" says Bushmen are his? Here we have just prepared the case for the *lekgota*. I want my goat.' The headman then instructed him to arrange for a trial by the *lekgota*, and the meeting ended.

When I asked the headman and the chief counsellor why they had not judged the case then and there, they said that while they had the authority to do so, they did not want the accused to have a chance to complain that he had been treated unfairly. And they cited an instance, five years old, of an assault case which the chief counsellor had heard without the *lekgota*. He had fined the defendant, who subsequently complained to the *lekgota* that he had not had a fair trial. (The *lekgota* increased the fine on the grounds that the defendant had 'despised' the chief counsellor.) This is certainly one reason for the rarity of extra-*lekgota* trials, and it had special cogency in this case since the chief counsellor was himself the plaintiff, but there are also other reasons which are important.

Political considerations move the headman and counsellors to prefer to involve as many citizens as possible in the judicial process. They often remark that they are afraid of being taken to task for decisions

---

[1] The English word, taken over from the police, is used.

reached on their own. Where citizens are on trial, there is the possibility of internal political repercussions if the hearing is not formal and public. If punitive action against a Bushman defendant is called for, the novel concern of 'Government' (who now claims to 'own' Bushmen) again leads the members of the village government to prefer a public trial. A trial by *lekgota* is not only the most legitimate, but it also spreads responsibility, and since the *lekgota* enjoys greater moral authority than any other body in the village its judgments are most acceptable to the losers.

The citizens, for their part, want to participate, not only to see that the trial is properly run but also because every case involves, in a sense, the interests of all the citizens. At one poorly-attended *lekgota* trial the complainant urged that 'Everyone should be present when the case is tried—tomorrow they [the accused] may kill someone else's cow'. It is not only one man's cow or goat that is at stake, people argue, but the common interest: it is therefore a *puo ya lekgota yo thyuna*, a matter for the great council.

This analysis is supported by an examination of one of the rare cases which was in fact judged by a judicial committee, without the *lekgota*.

The case of the abducted wife

A police patrol passed through Kuli one day, and a Naron Bushman took a complaint to one of the African constables—his wife had been abducted by a Ngologa man who came from Kalkfontein. The constable instructed him to take the matter to the headman, and it was tried on the same day. (The police were due to return within a day or two on their way back to their base.) The hearing took place near the headman's compound and was chaired by the headman. The chief counsellor, a popular counsellor and the schoolteacher (who just happened to be passing by) were the other members of the judicial committee.

The facts of the case were confused, but the committee was not particularly concerned to sort them out. Its main interest was in seeing whether the parties would accept a settlement of some kind. After some preliminary questioning the headman said: 'The case continues. The men in *kgota*[1] should question the person who brought the case.'

---

[1] Any public assembly, especially if chaired by the headman, may be called a *lekgota* or *lekgotana*, and the assembly-place is then termed *kgota* or *kgotana*. (The *-ana* suffix is diminutive.) However, the primary reference of these terms is to the central village assembly.

Chief counsellor: Who brought the case?
The girl's father: Sobe (the husband).
Chief counsellor: What do you want?
Sobe: I want my wife back.

Sobe was then questioned about his marriage, and his wife complained, 'I love Sobe, but he has other women.' The headman pressed Sobe, who said that if his wife came back to him he would be faithful. However, when the girl's father said he wanted to take his daughter away from both of the men, the headman sympathised with him.

Teacher (to the girl's father): How can you say such things? You did not bring this matter, it is Sobe's case. You said that the woman belongs to Sobe and now you are denying it.

Headman: Ask him why he is contradicting himself. Tell him to speak the truth.

The teacher put it to the girl's father that he had caused the original separation, and that was why he was now opposing Sobe. The popular counsellor warned the father that since he had not brought the case he should not speak too much. They wanted to restore Sobe's wife to him. If the father then found that Sobe was ill-treating her, he could report him.

The teacher then cross-examined the girl, who said that she was willing to return to Sobe. The teacher threatened all the parties with long terms of imprisonment for their various misdeeds, and told Sobe that 'After hesitating, after the persuasion of the *lekgota*, this woman has agreed to go with you. Now you must not take any more mistresses.'

The headman said that everyone present should speak. The popular counsellor urged the parties to accept the settlement, and then the headman pronounced judgment along the lines which had emerged. The defendant should release the woman and 'marry a Ngologa woman in his own village'. Sobe should stick to his one wife, and if he wronged her, her parents should bring him before the *lekgota*. The teacher led the cry of *Pula!* (Rain!) and the meeting ended.

The matter might never have been heard had the police not intervened, but this is not a sufficient explanation for the fact that a settlement was imposed without the *lekgota*. Three points are crucial here. (1) All the parties were outsiders. (2) As the plaintiff was a Bushman, nobody imagined that he might be awarded damages—and penal sanctions are rare in cases of this sort. (3) The parties were more or less agreed on what had to be done (the defendant was cowed by the intervention of the police), and so although there was some disagreement on the facts of the case, this was of minor importance. Thus although the headman would probably not have moved but for the police order (and in fact a previous complaint brought to a counsellor by the girl's father had come to nothing) he was ready now to act on his own initiative. If a citizen had been involved, if damages or penalties had been called for, or even had there been substantial disagreement, it is unlikely that he and the two counsellors would have been prepared to accept responsibility for settling the case. They would have insisted that it be taken to the *lekgota*, and done no more on their own initiative than carry out a preparatory investigation.

IV

In my introductory remarks I emphasised: (1) That the *lekgota*, in its role as a court, must be seen partly in relation to national agencies of law-enforcement; (2) that the *lekgota* deals with male citizens differently from minors or outsiders; and (3) that the jural structure of the agnatic corporation within the family-group is a crucial building-block of the legal system.

In the preceding pages I showed how these factors influence legal processes outside the *lekgota*. I shall now indicate the way in which they guide the *lekgota* in decisions about the admission of complaints and the arrangements for the hearing.

It is not too gross an oversimplification to say that where problems of jurisdiction and the admission of complaints arise, the *lekgota* responds in one of two ways. If the complainant is a citizen, or if a citizen is liable to penal sanctions,[1] the *lekgota's* reaction is, Why can't we hear this matter? In other cases the response is rather, Must we . . .? The answer to these questions depends largely on the *lekgota's* assessment of the probable reaction of the District Commissioner and the police. These considerations are likely to inhibit the headman more than the other citizens.

The case of the border theft

A Kuli citizen returning illegally across the border from South West Africa,[2] left some goods under a tree on the Botswana side before

[1] i.e. if a citizen is charged with a public delict, or if he is brought to court by an outsider or on the request of a Bushman.

[2] There is a regular illicit traffic of people and livestock between Botswana and South West Africa along the enormous and virtually empty frontier.

crossing again to fetch the balance of his possessions. On his return he found that some of his things had been stolen. Next morning he followed a spoor which led to the homestead of a fellow-citizen of Kuli, whom he then accused of the theft.

The *lekgota* was uncertain whether it had jurisdiction, even when it was established that the theft had occurred on the Botswana side of the border (about twelve miles from the village). The counsellor who had investigated the case was questioned by Mabote. 'Where were these things taken?' 'At the fence.' . . . 'Did the counsellors bring the matter before the headman, or the headman-in-*kgota*?' 'Before the headman—which means before the *lekgota* as a whole.' 'Did the headman accept the case?' 'We do not know. This is the first time it has been raised in the *lekgota*. The headman has not accepted it yet—only the *lekgota* members.' . . . 'The headman has said he would not take cases from the [border] fence but only matters arising in the village.' 'We acted because both parties are citizens of Kuli.' 'If people from Kuli commit an offence in South West Africa would you still hear the matter?' 'The headman has said that a boy or girl from Kuli who commits an offence in South West Africa [i.e. typically a young labour migrant] must be tried in Kuli.' 'The members of the *lekgota* will decide.'

Despite his general desire to hear all cases involving his subjects, the headman hesitated here since police from both sides of the border might be interested in the case, and the District Commissioner had indicated that smuggling and illegal border crossings were his concern. However, with the support of the members of the *lekgota* it was decided to apply the rule that their jurisdiction was over citizens rather than a geographical area.

Where jural minors—usually women or Bushmen—have a complaint, the *lekgota* generally takes the view that it should be presented by the complainant's legal guardian. But if the complainant goes to the District Commissioner or the police, the *lekgota* may be ordered to hear the matter. Usually it seeks an informal settlement. I have already cited *The Case of the Abducted Wife*, which was brought by a Bushman. The following two cases illustrate the reaction of the *lekgota* when mature, independent women brought complaints.

The case of the lady's cow

Kati was separated from her husband, Mabote. When her married son established his own family-group (near Mabote's but distinct from it), she went to live with him. Her son was later killed by a leopard while hunting, but his group continued its separate existence under Kati, who is the only woman group head in Kuli.

One day Kati came to the *lekgota* to complain about a poison-pen letter she had received from a woman in another village, and the *lekgota* praised her for taking this step. She then asked whether she might place another complaint before the meeting. A cow belonging to her had been caught in a trap by Bushman serfs of a citizen named Motobele, and she wanted compensation. The citizens were embarrassed by this request—Kati was behaving like a man! It was suggested that the matter be heard privately by the counsellors. A citizen asked whether Mabote still handled Kati's affairs. This was denied, although someone remarked that 'Once Kati had wanted to bring this matter to the *lekgota*, but her husband Mabote said he would take the necessary steps himself.' The headman commented that since the death of Kati's son it was Mabote's duty to look after her affairs, whether he maintained her or not. A counsellor supported this view, and said that a woman should take her complaints to a man by whom she had children, even if she was separated from him.

However, Motobele's younger brother, who was present, said that Motobele accepted liability, and a counsellor instructed him to see to it that Kati was compensated. Had Motobele's brother demurred, the *lekgota* would have been in a difficult situation. The indications from the debate are that the matter would have been referred to a counsellor for informal settlement outside the *lekgota*.

The case of the widow's field

An elderly woman, the associate of a family-group, economically independent, complained to a counsellor that the cattle of two prominent elders had on several occasions damaged her field. She failed to receive satisfaction—indeed her case was never seriously considered at any level. At last she took her complaint to the District Commissioner, and he referred it to the headman.

The headman brought the matter before the *lekgota*, which recognised, with some embarrassment, the implications of its masculine orientation. Citizens were more interested in cattle than in fields, which are largely the domain of women. Someone asked whether there was a 'Law of Fields', and was told that one was starting now. The headman's son said, 'we should take care of fields. A lady likes her field . . . but the field is ploughed by cattle! We buy seeds at the shop with [the proceeds of our] cattle. We buy clothes for our wives with cattle. Everything we do is by means of cattle!' A counsellor expressed dismay that people said they knew of no 'Law of Fields'—'you persecute your wives', he told the *lekgota*.

One citizen censured the counsellors for 'sending back' the complainant without redress. The case was at last heard, though with less formality than usual. The defendants conceded the case, and the headman ordered them to make restitution.

Despite the continual reference to the position of the District Commissioner and the police, these authorities do not necessarily determine the action of the *lekgota*, even if they order it to hear a matter. In one case, for example, when a visitor to Kuli had been robbed by Bushman guides (and after the headman's son had managed to recover most of the stolen goods), the European District police commander asked the headman to try the thieves. He said that if they were taken to the police-post for trial by the District Commissioner the case might be delayed for months. The District Commissioner would be likely to demand the presence of the complainant, who would by then probably have left, taking the goods in question. He felt that the headman would be able to try the matter in the absence of the complainant and the exhibits. Having explained this to the headman, he asked him what sentence he usually passed on Bushman thieves. The headman replied (with some exaggeration) that he always gave them five strokes each, and the officer commented that this was probably the best way of dealing with them.

The matter was raised and postponed on several occasions in the *lekgota*, and when it was finally discussed the *lekgota* decided that it could not reach a decision in the absence of the complainant. They collected statements to transmit to the police, and instructed the Lala leader to keep an eye on the accused until they could be handed over to the police. In short, partly because they were uncertain of the District Commissioner's reaction, but also on legal grounds, they demonstrated a concern for the niceties equal to that which the police officer had deplored in the District Commissioner.

The reluctance of the *lekgota* to act in these cases should be contrasted with its concern to settle matters brought by a citizen, or where a citizen is in danger of penal sanctions. The *lekgota* enjoys a fair measure of discretion, and where it chooses to judge a case the matter seldom goes further. Thus it can generally protect a citizen from outside intervention—even in an extreme case, as will be seen when I come to describe *The Case of the Cheeky Bushman*. Where the complainant is a citizen the *lekgota* also prefers to handle the case, partly in order to extract compensation, if this is possible. (The District Commissioner and police are more likely to impose penal sanctions, which do not help the complainant.) Here again the headman may be more willing than his subjects to hand over responsibility to the police.

One final point should be noted on the subject of jurisdiction. There are from time to time clashes of jurisdiction between two village courts. The rule is that a case is heard in the home *lekgota* of the complainant, but in the presence of delegates from the defendant's village. Sometimes, however, there is uncertainty about the domicile of one of the parties or some other impediment. In such situations the District Commissioner is usually asked to make a ruling. If a headman is brought to trial, the District Commissioner may order another headman to try his case.

v

Another set of problems about the admission of complaints and the arrangement of the trial stem from the structure of the jural corporation. In Ngologa law, a guardian of the defendant, often defined as the head of his family-group in the case of a citizen, should be present throughout a trial and is expected to assist the court. He will often also be held responsible for the payment of compensation or fines ordered by the court. If a Bushman is in the dock his master may play this role, although there is less pressure on him to do so, particularly since today it is often argued that 'Government' owns the Bushman. Similarly if a woman is on trial her guardian ('father' or husband) must be present, and he is held responsible for the payment of any levy imposed by the court. These rules ensure the execution of the court's orders, and, perhaps even more important, they harness the moral discipline of the family-group to the interests of the court. The identification of the legal guardian is therefore of primary importance, but it is not always straightforward, as for example when family-group associates are on trial.

The case of the sister's son

Masime's son and his sister's son were both accused of assault. His sister's son was the illegitimate child of an Herero man who had deserted the mother. The boy and his mother lived as associates in Masime's family-group. After the assault the boys ran away to South West Africa, and Masime told the *lekgota* that they had taken this course since he could not afford to pay fines on their behalf, and therefore they risked imprisonment.

A counsellor suggested that while Masime was liable for his son's fine, the *lekgota* should take the unusual step of making his sister responsible for the fine of the other boy, 'for the child obeys his mother, not his mother's brother'. He continued:

If the mother's brother writes to the boy he will not pay any attention, but he will if his mother writes, for she can say, I am your mother and father, and God also. The mother's brother can then write. The boy will see both letters and agree. If [the other accused, Masime's son] earns money while he is abroad, the money goes to his father, and therefore his father must pay the fine.

No authoritative ruling was made on this point, for the trial was postponed until the two boys should return to the village.

In another case the problem of legal guardianship was compounded by the possibility of a clash of jurisdiction between Kuli and Nojane.

The case of the jealous wife

A Ngologa man from the nearby village of Nojane had a Bushman mistress in Kuli. This upset his wife, who followed him to his mistress's place one day and beat her up. The headman and counsellors, together with some citizens, conducted a preparatory examination. Both the accused and her husband agreed to submit to a fine. However, one of the citizens who was present insisted that the father of the accused and other citizens of Nojane should attend the trial. A letter was accordingly sent inviting them to attend the forthcoming meeting of the *lekgota*.

When the case came before the *lekgota*, nobody from Nojane was present. A counsellor suggested that the *lekgota* go into the facts of the case but wait for the arrival of people from Nojane before embarking on a full trial. Other citizens questioned him about the preparatory examination, and some people suggested that the Nojane authorities would be quite content to allow the trial to proceed, without bothering to send representatives, since the accused was a well-known trouble-maker.

The headman's son said:

If I go [to Nojane] and commit an offence like this one now . . . some will say, Call his father. Others will say, Judge him, he did this on purpose— why did he leave his father? Now my father would be called, for Kuli and

Nojane are close to each other. If they were distant he would not be called, and I would just be judged. I did it, I know, for I am of the country. The law of today says this.

Counsellor: Hé! That person, isn't she the wife of S [who is present]? Well now, if a person is married, can she still say—should she be tried, perhaps, in Kalkfontein—saying, Where is my father?

Second Counsellor: We do not know. There is no rule. We must just try it and judge it. Her 'father' will be judged to be her husband.

This argument was accepted, and the trial proceeded, but not before the *lekgota* had assured itself once more that the accused and her husband were prepared to submit.

These cases illustrate some unusual problems in establishing who is responsible for the torts of a malefactor, and who should be present at his trial. There may be difficulties, however, even if all parties are citizens and members of family-groups.

The case of the brother's keeper

This case involved three full brothers, A, B and C. The youngest, C, sold a cow belonging to B to another villager, X. B was absent from the village on migrant labour at the time of the sale. On his return he repudiated it and took the cow back from X's kraal. X sued for its recovery.

In response to B's request, the *lekgota* stayed his trial until A could be present—A, the family-group head, was away on a visit to another village. When he returned, A remarked that he would have complained had the trial been held in his absence, 'for if a man is accused his "father" must be present—although the Europeans take only the accused'. Nevertheless he disclaimed any liability, on the grounds that B had contributed nothing to the family-group estate, and had even wasted some of A's assets.

Although the *lekgota* accepted A's argument—as one man said, 'If A refuses to pay his brother's fine we will say it is because his brother spoilt his property'—it insisted that B should make good X's purchase of his cow. The argument was not merely that the cow was B's, but that he had the responsibility of supporting his younger brother. B was asked, 'If you do not give your brother cattle who will support him? If you do not pay, there will be repeated cases in the *lekgota*'. At the same time, the *lekgota* refused to enquire whether C had the right to sell B's cow. This was a matter which should be referred to close agnates for settlement.

11

It should be noted that although B insisted on A's presence at the trial, A did not defend him; indeed, he made B appear in the worst possible light. Guardians are expected to support the *lekgota*, and any attempt to shield the defendant is immediately challenged. After making an initial statement they usually refrain from participation in the trial until the consensus has emerged, when they persuade their wards to accept the judgment of the *lekgota*.

VI

Trials which physically take place in the *kgota* before the headman and *lekgota* are characterised by greater formality and publicity and the more effective exercise of authority than other dispute-settling procedures in the village. More people attend such trials, and the village authorities are all expected to take part.

These trials generally involve at least one citizen. If the complainant is an outsider or a jural minor the case may be accepted only under pressure from the District Commissioner or the police. In any event, the *lekgota* will attempt to involve the legal guardian of the defendant in order to secure any levy imposed and to ensure the positive use of agnatic discipline.

Once the *lekgota* trial gets under way, the principles of compromise and conciliation, so prominent in domestic moots, fade into the background. Such a trial ends typically with a finding of liability followed by the imposition of a sentence. The decision is recorded for future inspection by the District Commissioner, reflecting the fact that the *lekgota*, in contrast to the village moots, has a dual frame of reference. It is at once at the apex of the village legal structure and at the base of the judicial system of the state.

A complaint is normally processed by a counsellor before it comes before the *lekgota*. The complainant takes his case to his family-group head (often via a 'father's younger brother'), who informs the nearest counsellor. A direct approach may be made to the other party to secure redress. If this fails the counsellor carries out a preparatory examination and brings the matter to the attention of the headman. The case is then put before the *lekgota*. It may be raised and postponed at several sessions until all the parties and their guardians, together with the witnesses and the village authorities, particularly the counsellors, can be brought together.

The procedure can then be broken down into five stages, although some may overlap or be telescoped. *First*, the problem is formally laid before the *lekgota*. The counsellor responsible for the case summarises the findings of the preparatory examination, if one has been held, and the parties make their statements. (Thereafter the protagonists and their guardians are usually disqualified from making further speeches, except in answer to questions. They may not cross-examine each other or the witnesses.) *Second*, the parties and perhaps the responsible counsellor are cross-examined by members of the *lekgota*, usually led by a counsellor. Witnesses may be called and examined, and other evidence—e.g. the hide of a stolen beast—is sometimes presented. (Witnesses are called by the court rather than by the parties.) The *third* stage emerges as the facts of the matter are established. The members of the *lekgota*, through informal commentaries, questions and speeches gradually agree on the areas of certainty and of doubt and reach some agreement on the merits. In the *fourth* stage the sense of the meeting is clearly formulated and the accused is invited to join the consensus by pleading guilty. In the final, *fifth*, stage the feeling of the citizens is transmitted through the decision-making hierarchy and fixed by the judgment. The case is 'given' to a counsellor, who sums up the views of the court and perhaps adds some observations of his own, and cites precedents. He then 'gives' it to the chief counsellor, who may similarly summarise the decision of the members of the court and add his own comments before he 'gives' the matter to (or 'prays') the headman. He often includes a plea for merciful treatment if compensation is not at stake. The headman then passes judgment and sentence. In his judgment he rarely departs from the consensus, though sometimes indicating his partial disagreement. Although he may intervene in the course of the hearing, he should not play too active a part until this final stage is reached.

The case of the cheeky Bushman

A Bushman named Sobe[1] was badly beaten up one night while at a drinking session in Waatotsi's compound. He appeared to be seriously injured, and some citizens thought he might die. In any event he would probably be taken to the Ghanzi hospital within a day or two, and it was likely that the police would then interest themselves in the case, perhaps arresting the Ngologa assailants. The general feeling was that the case should be heard at once, to stave off police intervention if possible.

---

[1] Sobe, it will be remembered, also figured in the *Case of the Abducted Wife*. He was, for a Bushman, very sensitive about defending his rights.

The *lekgota* assembled unusually early on the morning following the assault. There was an air of anticipation, and someone remarked that the headman was very happy because he saw wounds, and this gave him work. Seventeen men attended, aside from the plaintiff and myself. Waatotsi's wife and daughter were also present, sitting a little way from the men, waiting to give evidence.

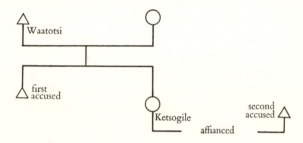

Fig. 7. Accused: *Case of the Cheeky Bushman.*

Immediately the *lekgota* had settled down the headman proposed to make a start. There was general agreement although the second accused had not yet arrived. Sobe was invited to tell his story. He said:

I was talking to the second accused when Waatotsi said I had been insulting. I said, if I have done something wrong, take me to the headman. The first accused said, Just beat the Bushman, and Ketsogile went and closed the gate [of the courtyard]. Then they beat me—the two accused and Ketsogile—with a stick. Waatotsi was telling them to kill the Bushman, he would pay, he had cattle. Even if my eyes could not see, my ears could hear who beat me. I ran to [a neighbour's] compound. I did not know where I was going. I came to the headman's village.

Sobe was then cross-examined by a counsellor, who tried to establish where each of the accused had hit and kicked him, and what they had said. Sobe kept referring to the second accused, and a citizen suggested that it was improper to continue the trial in his absence. However, other citizens were impatient to proceed. One man remarked, 'If Sobe dies they will go to gaol. Rather try the case and judge it.' The examination then proceeded.

Questions now focused on the cause of the incident. Sobe explained that the second accused had wanted Sobe to stand him to some drink. He had answered that 'if a Kgalagari man buys *khari* [a fermented drink] he doesn't give any to a Bushman, yet if a Bushman buys some he must give it to the Kgalagari man'. This had been taken as an insult and had provoked the assault. At this point a man was sent to summon the second accused immediately, for he had clearly been instrumental in the affair.

The first accused was then asked to make his statement. He said that Sobe had given adequate provocation, using insulting language about Kgalagari and even challenging the second accused to a fight. A citizen cautioned him: 'Give a clear statement to which [the second accused] will agree. Do not exaggerate.' He then completed his statement by saying that he had assaulted Sobe alone, and that only his father, Waatotsi, had been present. In cross-examination he was asked to clarify who had joined in the assault, but this time he said that it had been too dark to see.

A visitor from Nojane who had witnessed part of the incident backed up Sobe's story and testified that he had heard people saying, 'Kill the Bushman—a Bushman is worth nothing'. Other witnesses told conflicting stories. Ketsogile said that both the accused had assaulted Sobe, but that she had taken away a stick from the second accused, and had not taken part in the assault herself. Further attempts to get clearer admissions from the first accused, Ketsogile and their mother failed. When the second accused arrived at last he was asked to make a statement on which he was cross-examined. He too argued that Sobe had provoked the assault, but his story of the assault itself was confused.

The interest of the court gradually narrowed down to two questions: Who had struck Sobe? And where had he been hit? Sobe and the various suspects and witnesses were questioned again and again, over a period of several hours, on these two points. The general feeling was that others besides the two accused had participated in the assault, but this could not be proved.

When it was clear that the court could go no further, pressure was brought to bear on the two accused to persuade them to plead guilty. Although the second accused was unwilling to submit, the trial moved into its final stages. A citizen summed up:

[The first accused] said he kicked this man in the face, and Waatotsi and his daughter agreed. [The second accused] claims, however, that the Bushman started the fight. We must see the wounds, take witnesses and judge it. This wound is for [the first and second accused]. [The second accused] said that the Bushman hit him first, but [the first accused] disagreed. The headman should be given the case to judge.

The chief counsellor recalled a precedent. The headman of Kalk-fontein had himself been fined by his own *lekgota*, with his agreement, for inciting his son to assault a Bushman. The implication was that Waatotsi should also be held liable, although the chief counsellor did not spell this out. A counsellor urged, 'Counsellors, take time. You and the headman will take this case. The members of the *lekgota* have not spoken much.'

A final attempt was now made to implicate others in the assault, but without success. Further pressure was then put on the second accused to concede his guilt, and eventually he submitted. He was then told, 'you have given in to the members of the *lekgota*, they will give you to the headman'.

The headman passed judgment:

I am now tired, I will judge. [The first accused] admits that he kicked the Bushman. His sister said that [the second accused] also kicked the Bushman, and that [the first accused] punched him. [The second accused] admits that he kicked the Bushman.

Waatotsi does not advise his children against continually breaking the law. He is guilty. [To Waatotsi:] The fine is yours, yours and your children's. But the *lekgota* has refused. The *lekgota* has said that only two men are guilty.

The headman now jumped to his feet and began to pass sentence, but he was interrupted by the court-scribe, who insisted on reading a long and largely irrelevant passage from the Government *Gazette*. The headman listened in silence, and then said:

When I judge I do not judge as the whites do. The European judges for himself. I judge my people for myself, in my own country. The white place is in Ghanzi, because their camp is there. The Bible says, Judge honourably and blessedly. So I lead my people.

[First accused]—R10 or 2 years. [Second accused]—R10 or 2 years.[1] Now get the money or you will go to goal. *Re pula, Bangologa!*

And the citizens responded, *Pula!* (Rain!)

This case had several peculiar features (as has any case), but the broad procedure I outlined was followed. First came the plaintiff's statement, on which he was cross-examined, then the statement of the defendants, on which they were in turn cross-examined.[2] Had there been time this might have been done in a preparatory examination, and a counsellor would then have presented the findings to the *lekgota*. The *lekgota* might nonetheless have covered some of the same ground again. The

[1] The headman's court was not empowered to sentence anyone to two years' imprisonment; this was simply a threat to make the accused recognise the necessity of paying their fines.

[2] No oath or ordeal is taken by the parties or by witnesses.

court then focused its attention on the conflicts of evidence, and through cross-examination of the parties and the testimony of witnesses attempted to establish the facts. Several major uncertainties remained unresolved when at last a citizen (more usually a counsellor) summed up the agreed facts. It should be noted that while several people were 'in the dock' at the beginning of the trial, charges were at this stage being pressed only against the two young men. They were asked to admit their guilt. Finally the chief counsellor gave his opinion, backed by a precedent, and the headman pronounced judgment and sentence. In his judgment he followed the view of the court, while indicating his partial disagreement with it.

The fact that the complainant was a Bushman while the accused were citizens certainly affected the course of the trial. Had a citizen suffered the assault he would have demanded compensation, but since the Bushman are serfs, or even if they 'belong to "Government"' as the Ngologa now complain, they have no independent jural standing, and the assault was therefore treated as a penal matter. The fines were paid into the District Treasury and not paid to Sobe. The failure to press the case against Waatotsi, which as the chief counsellor and the headman indicated was quite reasonable, can similarly be ascribed to the statuses of the parties. Other aspects of the trial support the view that the court was not inclined to force the case against the defendants. Sobe claimed that he had been assaulted with a stick as well as by boots and fists, but although he displayed the stick marks on his back in response to a counsellor's request, this more serious charge was not pressed.

Nevertheless the trial was remarkable for its fairness in the circumstances. There was evidence of a concern for the law which overrode the desire to protect citizens. When the second accused appealed for leniency on the grounds that he was a citizen of the village, a counsellor demanded:

> Can a person of the country then do anything? Can one sentence one's own child? [The accused admitted that one could.] One can punish one's own son or daughter. If we sentence you, what will you do?
> *Second accused:* You always treat me harshly. I will agree if the guilt is placed on me by the *lekgota* . . . I cannot pay a fine because I am poor.
> *Counsellor:* If you are poor you should not keep making cases. You think you are strong and do not need others.

Finally, a pressing concern of the *lekgota* was to settle the case quickly, before it could be taken over by the police. The villagers acted in the hope that even if the case subsequently came to their attention, the police would not insist on a retrial by the District Commissioner.[1] Thus the *Case of the Cheeky Bushman* illustrates also the dual pressures on the *lekgota*, which must satisfy the citizens while taking account of the national system of law enforcement.

VII

In dealing with the second accused towards the end of the *Case of the Cheeky Bushman*, citizen spokesmen made explicit the notion that their job is to assess the guilt and secure the acquiescence of the accused, but that they then hand him over to the headman for judgment and sentence. In fact (as with judge and jury) the division of labour is seldom so clear. Headmen often intervene in a trial, and the citizens and counsellors make clear the kind of judgment they think appropriate. In practice the headman is usually guided by the consensus in formulating his judgment, but works out his own sentence.

Thus although the headman formally enunciates the judgment, and the counsellors play a leading role, the burden of judicial responsibility is spread widely. Both headman and citizens expect broad participation and an agreed decision. Cases are often postponed if counsellors or prominent elders with some interest in the matter are absent, and the village authorities are continually urged to make their views known. The emphasis on consensus is carried to the point where the acquiescence of the guilty person himself is demanded. Only if there is real disagreement is a case dropped, postponed, or referred to the police and District Commissioner. This last resort is used, as a rule, only if a man the *lekgota* considers guilty refuses to submit.

In the *Case of the Jealous Wife* a difficulty arose in the course of the trial which illustrates the demand that the judicial burden be shared. The counsellor responsible for the case was Mokgetise, Mabote's younger brother. However, for some reason he refused to play his role. At last another popular counsellor from his faction, Morimomongwe, took over the case, although at first he tried to evade the responsibility. He said:

We do not need to try the case [since the facts were not in dispute]. After the main points the case can be given to the chief counsellor. You should get the main points from Mokgetise. If he does not give the main points the

---

[1] Sobe was later taken to the Ghanzi hospital, where he was interviewed by the police, but they did not take any further action.

chief counsellor will not be able to handle the case. Only those two people are responsible.

Matlopelwe, the headman's son, pointed out that both the accused and her husband had pleaded guilty and accepted the jurisdiction of the *lekgota*. The citizens in the court agreed with him, and several voices urged Mokgetise to hurry up and do his job. Matlopelwe said, 'The counsellors should have said to the headman: The "father" of the woman has agreed, therefore judge, headman.'

The chief counsellor then attempted a summing-up:

Headman, there is no case. None. This person has been tried, and it is finished. Headman, the fault is that she injured the Bushman woman. The wounds are there. The woman followed her, she crossed the pan, she fought the Bushman woman in someone else's house. And now the headman should follow this and judge it. There is [the husband of the accused] who accepted the guilt.

However, the headman demanded that Morimomongwe should first tell him how to judge the case. Morimomongwe and Matlopelwe again questioned the accused, who once more admitted her guilt. Morimomongwe still hesitated, and said that the chief counsellor should help him. Matlopelwe went over the facts once more and argued that since they were so clear there was no cause to delay. At last Morimomongwe summed up:

Headman, your servants pleaded guilty and did not disapprove of the trial. [The husband] says he has long found himself guilty. That woman also says, I see the fault because when I did wrong I was not with my husband, and he also finds me guilty. *E re, ha e ja isiye marapo*—a maxim, When it (a lion) eats, it should leave the bones, i.e. they are poor, do not be too harsh.

Immediately Morimomongwe had committed himself the headman passed judgment. It is interesting to note that he talked as though the other popular counsellor from Mabote's faction, Mokgetise, had in fact done what was expected of him. After a brief preamble, he said:

[The husband] is liable, BaPebana, because here is the woman, she fought the Bushman woman while the Bushmen were dancing at Tatawane's place . . . The Bushman woman was pregnant, with child. I am not going to be harsh, because the counsellors have calmed me down. My counsellors take a case and give it to the chief counsellor. Then Mokgetise will say to the chief counsellor, Do you understand? Then the chief counsellor will stand up: Mokgetise says thus and thus, headman. But the chief counsellor has been calmed down by Mokgetise.

And he then passed sentence.

The most interesting aspect of this emphasis on full participation and agreement is perhaps the demand that the guilty party plead guilty and accept the judgment of the court. As I have said, this is often effected through the mobilisation of agnatic discipline. When the second accused hesitated to plead guilty in the *Case of the Cheeky Bushman*, his father intervened and said, 'I am the father and therefore I cannot be my own witness. M. is a habitual offender. The headman has warned him but he has not heeded. How can we help him if he does not listen to advice? He should not pay so many visits but rather remain at home more.' And under this pressure the man at last admitted his guilt.

In the *Case of the Border Theft* this mechanism failed, and the *lekgota* was forced to abandon the case. There was a great deal of circumstantial evidence pointing to the accused. Further, he had behaved in an uncooperative manner during the preparatory examination, and had refused to allow the counsellors to search his hut.

The accused insisted that his elder brother should attend the trial, but when the trial began it became evident that the elder brother would not cooperate with the court. He was warned that 'at a session of the *lekgota* one must not act on behalf of another person or one will be charged with him'. The headman said:

Everyone should take care of what I am going to say in the *kgota*. These people are crooks. The *lekgota* should not be defeated by the accused. You should question them thoroughly. If you are unable to try this case, you should refer it to those who can [i.e. the police].

Both the accused and his brother were subjected to further examination, but they refused to give way. At last the junior of the two counsellors who had been responsible for the preparatory examination asked the senior what steps he intended to take. The senior answered that the headman should take the case to the local police station-commander. The headman then said, 'Since K. has not admitted his guilt we should not find him guilty, but rather take the matter to the station-commander'. The headman's brother, Mabote, commented, 'I thought K. would plead guilty. There is only one law for the headman and the District Commissioner.'

VIII

When he comes to pass sentence the headman may choose one or more of a variety of sanctions. He may order compensation or damages in kind or in cash, and if he wishes to impose a penal sanction he can order the payment of a fine or imprisonment or thrashing. He may also reprimand the guilty party. Sometimes different sanctions are combined. Many sentences are backed by what might be called a reserve sanction, which comes into force if the restitution or penal fine is not paid. The reserve sanction is usually imprisonment. In some cases the headman orders the payment of restitution and in addition a penal sanction, usually a fine but sometimes a thrashing.

The normal penal sanction is a fine, and generally fines and orders of restitution are made in money terms. They rarely go as high as R30, usually falling between R4 and R20, the headman relating the levy as a rule to the wealth of the party. Restitution is sometimes levied in livestock, but this may be commutable into a cash payment. Traditionally penal fines were payable in stock and distributed in the *lekgota*. Today they are generally levied in cash terms, and are paid into the Tribal Treasury.

The imposition of a reserve sanction of imprisonment is usually regarded as a threat, an earnest of the kind of action which might be taken if the initial order is not carried out. The Ngologa prefer any sanction to imprisonment, and most of them can realise enough cash to pay their fines if necessary.

In the general run of cases the choice of sanction is determined by the status of the parties rather than the nature of the offence. If a citizen is the complainant, restitution is generally ordered, and if the defendant in such a case is a Bushman he is likely to be threatened with imprisonment or a thrashing in order to squeeze compensation from him. (This happened, for example, in the *Case of the Hungry Bushman*.) A Bushman complainant, on the other hand, is rarely awarded compensation or damages. Women and outsiders form an intermediate category, who may be awarded restitution. As a rule, however, complaints brought by such parties end with the imposition of a penal sanction. Occasionally the community itself mounts an action, or intervenes as a party in a matter brought by a citizen, particularly in assault cases. Where this happens penal sanctions are ordered, sometimes in addition to restitution. If penal sanctions are ordered against a citizen, a sentence of imprisonment is usually avoided. Non-citizens are more readily sent to prison.

The range of sanctions available to the *lekgota* might be divided into those which depend on the police for enforcement and those which do not—although the threat of police sanctions may back up others.

Similarly, two distinct sets of pressures operate on a citizen who has been ordered to pay a fine, compensation or damages. He is constrained to pay the levy by the fear of imprisonment or thrashing by the police, and also by the pressure of public opinion and the persuasion of his close kin, particularly the members of his family-group. In 1964, I witnessed in Kuli a full-scale campaign to make some dilatory offenders pay their fines, and I was able to see how the dual pressures, from within and without the village, are brought to bear on the offenders and on the village authorities.

The case of the unpaid fines

The campaign was sparked off by a letter which the court-scribe wrote to the District Commissioner. In it he complained that some villagers had not paid the fines imposed on them by the *lekgota* within a reasonable time. The District Commissioner sent the police to investigate, but the headman turned them back, asking them to give his people time to collect their fines. The members of the *lekgota* criticised the court-scribe for his action, which he had taken without consultation. He defended himself on the grounds that his job demanded it. The citizens then turned to the defaulters.

Various arguments were advanced to persuade the defaulters to pay. One was a counsellor, and he was asked how others could be expected to settle their fines if the counsellors did not. He paid. In the case of other, younger, men, pressure was exerted on the fathers. The headman, for example, said at one stage:

Mokwe also has not paid his fine. Ask his father to pay. We have considered this for a long time. We must give these people to the police. Those who are away—their fathers must come and explain this to the District Commissioner.

The citizens were concerned with the threat of anarchy if men could escape sentences imposed by the *lekgota*. Speaker after speaker made this point at meetings. It was perhaps put most forcibly by Waatotsi:

In Kuli everyone does as they like. There is no headman and no counsellors . . . In other villages the guilty are just fined. They are not first asked whether they can afford it. The headman must get Government's help if the tribe does not respect him.

But the headman refused to take the responsibility of unilateral action. He demanded the support of the *lekgota* before calling in the police. A counsellor put the point succinctly:

There are five *kgota's* [in Ghanzi District]. Men are thrashed in Tšekwe's *kgota* [Kalkfontein] but not in Ramoŝwane's or Keakopa's [Kuli and Nojane]. Here people drink *khari* and destroy the *kgota*. They have knives and would knife any man who tried to thrash them. Will we give R to the police tomorrow? And when he takes out his *kierie* [club] we will say, No, it is the headman who called the police, go and club him. Therefore the headman asks these questions, to allow us to arrest them.

At last only two men remained who would not pay their fines. (I except R. The *lekgota* was too frightened to move against him.) Their fathers acquiesced in calling the police, and a consensus was achieved for this drastic measure. The police came to the *kgota*, and the headman gave the two defaulters a choice of a thrashing or imprisonment. They chose to be whipped. The sentence was carried out in the *kgota* by a counsellor in the presence of police and citizens.

A review of this campaign brings out the importance, in the last analysis, of the police sanction. It also shows that the more traditional processes, the operation of public opinion and the manipulation of senior agnates, are still important. Finally, the campaign shows once more the importance for the headman of achieving a consensus before taking action. In this case a consensus was achieved because the village government was faced with the District Commissioner's demand for action, and because the citizens themselves are so strongly committed to the maintenance of their judicial authority.

Nevertheless the system is not always efficient. Domestic pressures may fail if a man is not tightly enmeshed in village relationships. Alternatively, the *lekgota* may feel that it simply lacks the authority to coerce certain men. R, for example, was not pressed for the fines he owed. He was feared as a violent man, and had no close kin among the elders who could exert pressure on him. Nor was there any attempt to coerce an alien schoolteacher, who had been transferred to another village after a series of court-cases as a result of which he owed several fines.

Further, a citizen complainant is often reluctant to see the police called in, for he then loses the chance of compensation or damages with the execution of the reserve sanction. There is often no real solution to this problem. I have described the *Case of the Brother's Keeper*. When I returned to Kuli two years after the trial, X had still not recovered his purchase. I questioned the headman about this and he explained that brother A had failed to persuade his younger brother, B, to restore the cow with its progeny. When I remarked that A himself might be held responsible, the headman said that the *lekgota* was afraid to oppose such an influential man. The headman also stressed that this was a difficult case to handle since the *lekgota* is chary of interfering between brothers. He added that X would probably bring the matter before the *lekgota* once more when he returned from his present extended visit abroad.

The sub-chief of Hukuntsi is never troubled by the anxieties which face his colleagues in these situations. He favours imprisonment for many offences, and since he rules with police backing he can dispense with the approval of his subjects. Nor do problems of this sort arise in any of the villages when Bushmen are sentenced by the *lekgota*. After attempting to extort restitution the *lekgota* readily turns them over to the police for punishment, or arranges for them to be thrashed.

IX

Three themes have constantly recurred in this chapter: (1) the key role of agnatic corporations and discipline in the system; (2) the different legal status (in various contexts) of adult male Ngologa as opposed to outsiders, women and Bushmen; and (3) the interaction of national and community interests and institutions in the process of the administration of the law.

(1) The family-group and family-group alliance may form the basis of a kinship moot. They provide the core of participants, the context of values, and the authority structure. A moot may also be based on the sub-clan, but it does not have the persuasive power of the agnatically based small-scale kinship moot and it may be regarded as a threat by the headman, and lack political legitimacy.

The *lekgota* makes use of the kinship structure in various ways. The corporate structure of the family-group permits a form of representation for parties to a dispute, and allows the *lekgota* to hold senior citizens responsible for the torts of those over whom they enjoy paternal or quasi-paternal authority. These elders also bolster the authority of the *lekgota* by using their own kinship statuses to bring younger, perhaps less responsible men to accept the *lekgota*'s judgments.

The structure of kinship relations in the village may be said in these ways to be fused with the legal system, though without compromising the objectivity of the *lekgota*, at least when the parties to a case are citizens. The dependence on consensus ensures that the kin of office-holders cannot be favoured as against other citizens. A consequence of this use of kinship authority, however, is that the *lekgota* cannot cope with affairs involving close agnates, particularly if they are members of one family-group.

(2) The integration of the kinship structure with the legal system is only effective where citizens and their women and children are concerned. This is one reason for the different treatment accorded Bushmen and other outsiders. More generally, all the citizens are members of the *lekgota*, and so a citizen who is involved in a case stands in a different relationship to the court than does an outsider.

Where the complainant is a citizen, the first aim of the court is to secure restitution. If a citizen is the defendant, there is a strong desire to enforce the law without resort to the police. Non-citizens (including independent women) may call upon the District Commissioner or the police to ensure that their complaints are dealt with, but the *lekgota* is less likely to award them damages or compensation. And if the defendant is a non-citizen, the *lekgota* is readier to use the coercive powers of the state, particularly if the defendant is unable or unwilling to make restitution.

(3) The state, whether colonial or post-colonial, does not effectively supervise the legal process in the villages. There is no real need to do so, for the national élite is excluded from the jurisdiction of the village courts.[1] The concern of the state has been simply to ensure that 'law and order' are maintained. But implicit in this has been the demand that the headman and his court should serve everyone, and not only citizens. Therefore increasingly in recent years the state has limited the extent to which citizens can use their dominant position to secure their interests in the courts. Another limiting factor has been the Ngologa ideology of the rule of law, which makes citizens and counsellors take an altruistic stand at times, as is apparent in some of the cases I have described.

Further, the state provides the ultimate sanctions for the decisions of the *lekgota*, and by its very presence it makes the *lekgota* more likely to reach consensus on a measure which will allow the defendant to be dealt with by the villagers.

x

Some points of theoretical interest remain to be discussed. It is remarkable that the *lekgota* almost inevitably finds the defendant at fault,

---

[1] In colonial times the village courts did not have jurisdiction over Europeans and Coloureds, although such people might submit to a ruling of the *lekgota* rather than be taken before the District Commissioner. The educated elite lives mainly in the towns, and in any case is privileged to by-pass the customary courts if they wish to do so.

although sometimes the complainant may also be reprimanded or even punished (particularly in assault cases). The main reason for this is that most cases arise in the village, which is a small and intimate community, and so the facts of the matter and the background to the case are usually well-known to the members of the *lekgota*. It is difficult to hide anything in this sort of community, but at the same time an innocent person is unlikely to be suspected of a misdemeanour. The preparatory examination further sifts out the dubious accusations before they come to court, reducing once again the chances of a finding of not-guilty. For example, in the *Case of the Hungry Bushman*, the case against the Lala children was dismissed in the preparatory examination, and only the thief himself was taken before the *lekgota*. Finally, in contrast to the situation reported in some other legal systems, malicious prosecutions are rare. It is difficult to see how they could succeed, given the structure of the *lekgota*.

It is perhaps less easy to explain why the defendant is usually found liable and ordered to make restitution. Only in kinship moots is the emphasis on compromise and conciliation. This might be regarded as dysfunctional. For one thing, ensuring that the court's levy is paid is often time-consuming and not always certain. Further, it might be argued (and this is implicit in some of Gluckman's writings) that within a small-scale community ongoing social relationships are best maintained by a conciliatory judgment.

The answer may be along the following lines. Attempts are made to settle the dispute before it comes before the *lekgota*; and if there are ongoing ties of kinship, affinity or neighbourly cooperation between the parties, an agreed compromise may well be negotiated. But the *lekgota* itself is not in a good position to press for an amicable settlement. It lacks the necessary detachment, on the one hand, and on the other it cannot appeal to the values of kith and kin since it operates within the politico-jural domain.

Gluckman has written of the Lozi *kuta* that it 'tends to be conciliating; it strives to effect a compromise acceptable to, and accepted by, all the parties'. He suggests that this is because:

For them it is a supreme value that villages should remain united, kinsfolk and families and kinship groups should not separate, lord and underling should remain associated. Throughout a court hearing of this kind the judges try to prevent the breaking of relationships, and to make it possible for the parties to live together amicably in the future. (1955: 20–1.)

But the crucial feature of the courts with which Gluckman dealt is precisely that they were high-level courts, detached from the multiplex relationships in which the parties were enmeshed. The members of the *lekgota*, on the contrary, are typically closely involved with the parties, and the *lekgota*'s authority and its whole ethos depends on the transcendance of domestic ties and values in favour of more generalised and impersonal political relationships. The *lekgota*'s strength is in its objectivity and strict legalism.

But this does not necessarily mean that fellow-villagers divided by a law-suit are never reconciled, or that offenders are not reintegrated in the community. The maintenance of social relationships (or their adjustment) is achieved through the submission of the offender and the payment of restitution. The *lekgota*'s reluctance to use the police to coerce citizens must be related in part to their desire to persuade the offender to submit, so that he can be quickly reintegrated into the complex of social relationships.

9

CONCLUSION

I

The framework of village politics may be reviewed briefly. To begin with the internal environment of the village political system—the village community is made up of a series of kin-based local groupings: the family-group, family-group alliance and sub-clan. The family-group, a set of households under the leadership of an elder, constitutes the most cohesive social unit in the community. At its centre is a corporation of male agnates, recruited mainly from among the sons and brothers of the group head. A family-group alliance is made up of several neighbouring family-groups whose heads are normally close agnates. The sub-clan (which is made up of the members of a particular clan who live in the village) may be co-extensive with a family-group alliance. However, it is sometimes not a solidary group, containing instead two or more opposing family-group alliances.

Members of a family-group usually separate and form new groups when the head dies, or when his sons or brothers marry and their sons reach maturity. These new groups sometimes form alliances, which may be strengthened or created by agnatic cousin marriages. However, even the overlay of affinal and matrilateral ties is often not enough to contain the process of fission, and in many cases the new groups stand in opposition to each other. The fission of the leading family-group in an alliance may precipitate more far-reaching disruption, and bring about a wholly new pattern of alliances and oppositions within a sub-clan. The consequences which follow the death of a headman are particularly important, and mark a watershed in the development of alliances and oppositions within the village.

Women and children are treated as minors in political and jural contexts. So are the Bushmen who are often attached to Bantu villages in the Kalahari. With the occasional exception of elderly and independent women, these people have access to the political institutions of the community only through their fathers, husbands or masters, or as a result of intervention by the District authorities.

In addition to the dominant ethnic group, whose structure I have outlined, and their dependents, a village may contain a minority Bantu group. Such a group operates rather like a sub-clan, but its members participate less fully in public affairs than do the men of the core community.

The central political institutions in the village are the *lekgota* and the headmanship. Those adult men who enjoy full political rights, the citizens, meet regularly as the village assembly, the *lekgota*. This body makes or reviews all major political decisions. It is dominated by a small circle of men, the village authorities, to which all the office-holders and some private citizens belong. Some of the headman's leading opponents are normally members of this group.

The *lekgota* is always split into two or more factions, led by members of the village authority. They are based on the co-residential kinship groups within the village, and consequently their structure alters with developments in the sphere of kinship relationships in the village. The factional structure of the ruling sub-clan is radically altered by every succession crisis, when one group of the old headman's family breaks away to oppose the successor.

The village government is led by the headman, who is chosen on a semi-hereditary basis. He does not enjoy great authority, and depends upon general support for the implementation of any decision, which should thus command a consensus. Of his counsellors, some, usually including the chief counsellor, are his own men, often close relatives, committed to his support. The balance of the counsellors serve him administratively but are expected to check any tendency to authoritarian or unconstitutional action on his part. Their main constituency is within the citizen body, and counsellors are normally drawn from each sub-clan or major faction.

The most important institutions in the 'external environment' of the village political system are the District authorities and the Democratic Party. The relationship with the District headquarters determines much of the content of village politics and exercises a pervasive influence on the conduct of politics. Since the 1930s there has been a tendency towards greater centralisation of District administration. The village has been drawn progressively more tightly into the local government structure, and the role of the headman has been redefined from above. At the same time, the *lekgota* has become more preoccupied with 'development' issues, which demand District-level aid, a reflection of the growing involvement of the villagers in wider administrative, political and economic relationships.

12*

Until recently, communication between the District authorities and the village was effectively one-way. Orders came from above, but demands from below were not regularly, nor usually successfully, transmitted to the superior authorities. However, the District Commissioner was not a successful autocrat. Since there was a serious lack of mutual comprehension, and because the resources of the District were over-extended, his impact on village politics was neither consistent nor well-managed. Nevertheless, ultimate power was with the District Commissioner, and in virtually every political context the villagers trimmed their sails to the winds they sensed from District headquarters. They were always aware that the District authorities might intervene when they were holding a trial, or formulating a policy or competing for power; and that they could enforce a particular line of action or hold the village government responsible for some past decision. The successful invocation of the District Commissioner by a village faction could be a decisive political manoeuvre in some situations.

A change in this state of affairs came with Botswana's independence and the establishment of predominantly elective District Councils in 1966. District administration was not fundamentally politicised (although this was a temporary effect) but communication between District headquarters and the villages improved. The 'new men' of the District became the communication-brokers. They transmitted village demands to the new District Council and to the District Commissioner, and carried policy-decisions back to the villages. They immediately acquired influence at headquarters, and, partly in consequence, were able to take the lead in much of the village's policy-making activities. They avoided identification with any of the kin-based factions, and were often able to break the deadlocks which resulted from factional conflict. In short, they introduced a new purposiveness and efficiency into village government. It is above all their impact which accounts for the contrasts between the pre-Independence and post-Independence situation at this level of political life.

The Botswana Democratic Party, which moved into the Kalahari in the early 1960s, served a vital role in this transformation. They recruited the 'new men', the rising entrepreneurs, into the Party and made them leaders of the District, eventually allowing them to institutionalise their new roles as District Councillors. Using these men, the Party also prepared the villagers for participation in District and even national affairs, and set up an organisational structure which has persisted.

11

Support for the village political system comes both from the citizens and the powers external to the village. This support is directed to (*a*) the village government and authorities; (*b*) the constitutional arrangements; and (*c*) the political community itself.

(*a*) The headman is supported by the community so long as he does not consistently attempt to overrule the views of the citizens or promote the interests of his faction too narrowly. He depends on this support, for the alternative, the backing of the District authorities, is not consistent or adequate. The exception to this rule, the Hukuntsi sub-chief, is able to sacrifice popular backing because there is a subservient police-station at hand, a most unusual situation. Any headman, however, may rely on the external authorities in some situations, though at the expense of domestic support.

The village authorities as a group can lead the villagers because they are senior members of the major corporate groups within the community, and, often, the most experienced and able politicians. If the authorities are divided among themselves, support is split. Each kin-based faction then supports its own leading members against other members of the village authority. In general the source of an issue, and its subject-matter, determine the pattern of support.

(*b*) The village constitution—the ideology of the political system— is expressed in a few partial models. First, the villagers recognise the constraints and opportunities which follow from the local government system. They accept that the legitimacy of the headman derives to some extent from recognition by external authorities, and that village affairs must be governed with reference to the overarching structure of the state. Secondly, they represent the headman as the ultimate decision-maker, though he should accept the guidance of his citizens and the counsellors. Thirdly, the political system is sometimes seen in quasi-kinship terms. The founding sub-clan has special rights in the running of the village. The headman and the leading counsellors derive their authority from their positions as members of the senior line of the founding sub-clan. Members of junior sub-clans, like younger brothers, can advise but should obey and serve their seniors. At the same time, however, people contrast the claims of kinship with the often conflicting rights and duties of citizenship. Indeed, the headman is severely criticised if he is thought to favour his kin, particularly in legal matters.

Although more democratic ideas are sometimes expressed, the Ngologa tend to represent their political system in formal terms as authoritarian and traditional, yet open to popular influence; consistent with the kinship system, yet free of bias or conflict—briefly, as a paternalistic and hierarchical system. This is not to say that the Ngologa do not appreciate the realities of village politics. Their political behaviour reflects practised understanding, and so do many of their informal comments, which are often phrased as complaints about the ways in which a particular village government falls short of the ideal. These political theories, rightly understood, are sources of legitimisation of the existing political arrangement. It may seem paradoxical that a highly democratic political system should be supported by authoritarian values; although, after all, the contrary situation is not uncommon. The point is that they serve to bolster the minimum authority which the system uses, and help to articulate the village political system with the domestic organisation, on the one hand, and with the national government on the other.

Another source of support for the system follows from the broad agreement of the citizens and the Government on the goals of community action. The political system has always been able to realise some of these goals, and although inefficient in many spheres, it remained the only credible form of political machinery. Until the emergence of the District Councillors, no alternative system presented itself —the most serious challenge was that new, younger headmen should be appointed. Today the District Councillor is accepted as a leading member of the dominant group, and his presence has led to an improvement in the efficiency of the political system in processing and meeting demands.

(c) The integrity of the political community was often challenged by secessions in the early decades of the present century. Today it is far more secure. Government defines the village as a unit of local administration, and this external definition helps to contain fission. Fission is further restrained by the common desire to be near schools, boreholes, roads and stores.

Occasionally there are moves to enlarge the political community. The Ngologa of Kuli have considered intervention in the affairs of Nojane, where a Ngologa majority is ruled by Tlharo. For many years the headman of Lehututu claimed sovereignty over Kuli, which was colonised by his kinsmen. However, Government has frustrated all such irredentist policies. The only successful modification of the village-based polity was introduced by Government itself—the Northern Kgalagadi sub-chieftaincy, which embraces five villages.

The introduction of demands into the village political system—like support—must be traced both to citizen interests and to the interests of the external authorities. To begin with, environmental factors limit the type of matters which become political issues. The affairs of corporate kinship groups and of religious groups are as a rule excluded from the purview of the political institutions. The affairs of women and of Bushmen are considered only under special circumstances. For their part, the District authorities settle many issues without consulting the villagers, and they may withdraw some issues from the village arena. But despite these limitations, the villagers regulate a wide range of affairs through their political institutions.

First, disputes between members of different groups are settled, and offenders against the community are dealt with. Secondly, the affairs of the village as a corporation are transacted, and the machinery of government is kept in order. Under this head come the demands of segments of the community for a special share in jobs or influence; demands which can succeed only through political competition with similar segments.

Thirdly, the villagers' demands are transmitted to the District authorities, and the relationship of the village with these external authorities and the Party is regulated. This is a very important area of activity. Villagers are concerned to limit Government interference in their affairs, while at the same time gaining a share of the goods distributed from District headquarters. Many economic demands cannot be satisfied within the framework of village government, but it is in the power of the District authorities to grant vital concessions to the interests of pastoralism, agriculture, migrant labour and hunting. Demands relating to schooling are also normally beyond the power of the village authorities to meet, and here again the main thrust is towards putting pressure on the District authorities. The great events of the 1960s, the drought and the coming of Botswana's independence, broadened the range of issues which involved the villagers with external authorities.

Fourthly, the external authorities may also make demands on the village authorities. They expect the village leaders to maintain a certain level of competence in dealing with internal policy and judicial matters. At the minimum, the village must be kept running without undue resort to the District Commissioner or the police on the part of the village authorities or disgruntled individuals. But they may also expect the village authorities to carry out certain tasks, even to administer policies, on their behalf.

Finally, the emergence of the 'new men' in District and village politics created new pressures, particularly after Botswana's independence. The new District Councillors tended to be impatient of the old style of village politics. They demanded greater efficiency and initiative, and in general a more authoritative conduct of village affairs.

III

The structure I have described might be represented diagrammatically (Fig. 8).

I have indicated the main features of the political system and its environment, and discussed the 'inputs' (in the form of support and demands) from the environment to the political system. It remains to examine, first, the decision-making process; and then the feed-back from the political system to its environment.

The decision-making process in the *lekgota* takes three main forms, each of which is associated with a characteristic category of issues. I begin with judicial matters, which are processed with greater formality than other sorts of issue. These matters are normally initiated by one private party, which brings the other to court. Typically, the court is cohesive during the judicial process, the parties are isolated, and senior agnates of the defendant are used to persuade him to submit to the judgment, and to guarantee the execution of the sentence. Particularly where the parties are citizens, the members of the court have a common interest in securing a just decision and the capitulation of the loser. The police and District Commissioner can almost always be counted upon to support the judgment. Under these circumstances, decisions are normally consensual and moderately easy to enforce.

Secondly there are the issues which involve the villagers as a group with external authorities. They may press demands upon the District authorities, or be required to administer policies emanating from above, or which result from a dialogue between the villagers and the external authorities. The general aims of both villagers and the external authorities often coincide, but even if the villagers resent a decision imposed upon them they cannot effectively oppose it. In any case, the villagers normally present a united front when they deal with external authorities. Internal political conflicts are likely to arise only if the villagers are

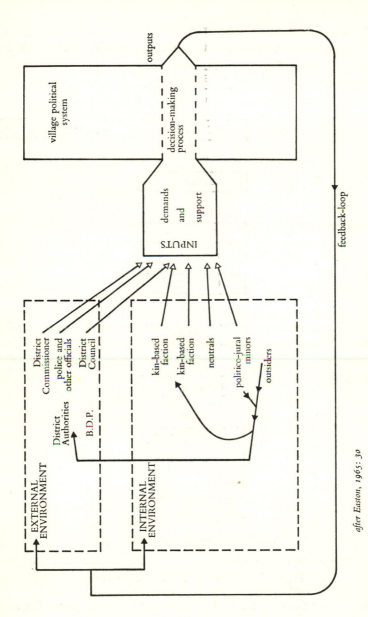

Fig. 8. The political system.

after Easton, 1965: 30

given wide discretion in the implementation of a policy. The decision-making process is then similar to that which is generated by internal policy matters.

The third set of issues concern internal policy, a category which covers matters of internal administration, jobs and authority. In dealing

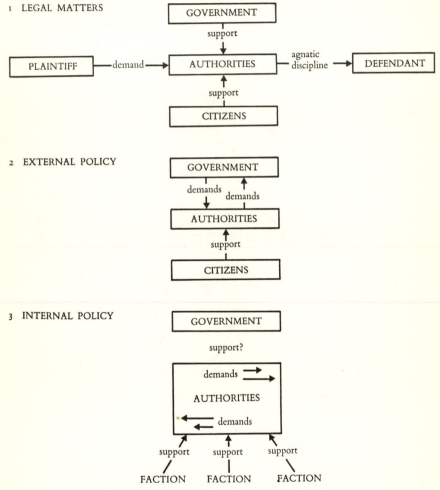

N.B. 'Government' refers to the District Authorities   'Authorities' means the village authorities

Fig. 9. The structure of demands and support.

with matters of this sort, the *lekgota* is often split into factions. A temporary resolution may be reached if two factions combine against a third, particularly if the majority successfully invokes the support of external authorities.

Each set of issues is associated with a particular form of decision-making process because the type, origin or direction of a demand generates an appropriate support structure. In most legal cases the parties are isolated. The citizen body is united and impartial. The external authorities are always ready to lend support to the cause of 'law and order'. The pressures are therefore adequate to guarantee sufficient support to the authorities and the mode of action. Where the villagers confront external authorities they are themselves usually united and agreed upon their goals. Their spokesmen have full support. In internal policy-matters, however, the demands come from a section of the authorities, supported by their factions, and are directed against other factions. Support is segmentary, and unless one faction can gain the backing of external authorities, it is extremely difficult to get an effective decision to take positive action.

The argument may be summarised in diagram form (Fig. 9), on the opposite page.

I V

The decision-making process is the political system in action, and it may be worthwhile briefly to turn from the rather abstract considerations of the last few pages to some of the cases I cited in the text, in order to recall the way in which the system works in practice.

Legal issues

The factors making for consensus and a workable decision are the backing of outside authorities, the unity of the court as against the parties, and the use of agnatic discipline in compelling the submission of the defendant. The crucial role of these factors is immediately apparent when one fails: as agnatic discipline did in the *Case of the Border Theft*, where the defendant's elder brother sided with him and the court was forced to refer the matter to the police. The unity of the court is likely to be threatened only in a politically-motivated trial. These are rare, however, and although some were reported to me, I never witnessed one. The support of the outside authorities is steady, but it should be noted that where the plaintiff is not a citizen this support may be directed to the plaintiff rather than to the court—at least potentially. This possibility was of major importance in the *Case of the Cheeky Bushman*. A consideration of this case brings to mind a further factor which is central to Ngologa politics—the high cultural valuation of law and of legal processes. These concerns helped to prevent the trial of Sobe's assailants from being a travesty.

External policy

Often the *lekgota* is simply ordered to communicate a routine decision made at District headquarters, or to supply some information. Sometimes, however, dealings with external authorities generate political activity in the village, usually when some initiative is demanded of the villagers. In such situations, confronted directly with the external authorities, the members of the *lekgota* normally close ranks.

One such situation arose when the police came to Kuli to arrest the villagers who had not paid fines ordered by the *lekgota*. Their intervention was the result of a letter from the court-scribe to the District Commissioner. The villagers were incensed by the court-scribe's action, but abandoned this domestic quarrel in order to solve the immediate problem—they had no wish to let off the defaulters, but they did not want to condemn them to imprisonment. Their patient and united search for a satisfactory domestic resolution illustrates the cohesion of the villagers in the face of a potentially dangerous demand from outside. But they will also present a united front when they want something positive from the external authorities.

The question of the expansion of the school, for example, was advanced in an amicable dialogue between the District Commissioner and the village authorities. The villagers accepted the necessity of making their contribution to the project, and were able to reach swift agreement on the way in which the levy should be raised. The village authorities unitedly urged on their fellow-citizens, emphasising always the necessity of impressing the District Commissioner with their zeal in this matter . . . Unfortunately, the project almost fell through in the end, because of failures in communication between the District Commissioner and the village.

Internal policy

In many matters of internal policy the *lekgota* is divided and the external authorities do not consistently support any faction. In these circumstances a decision *not* to act can be reached if two factions combine against a third; but a decision to take positive action is uncommon unless the majority can get the direct support of the District authorities. Such support is unlikely to persist, however, and so the resolution may not be lasting.

In the affair of the *Headman and the Counsellor*, the headman tried to take action against a Silebe counsellor. This implied both a move to extend his own authority and a challenge to the whole Silebe group. In the course of the debate a successful constitutional defence was advanced, and not only did the opposition Pebana faction side with the Silebe, but even close supporters of the head-man showed that they were unhappy about his high-handed action. The intervention of a visitor allowed the headman to abandon an untenable position.

The case of the *Borehole and the Pumpers* illustrates how difficult it is to reach an agreed decision if an issue touches on internal power or jobs; and how frangible any decision to act will be if based merely on majority support, even if the majority includes the headman and is backed at some stage by the District Commissioner. It will be remembered that the affair passed through three main phases. *Round 1:* Morimomongwe, the pumper, left Kuli and installed his son Sekoma as his successor. Presently Sekoma went on strike because he had not been paid. The headman used Silebe support to displace Sekoma (who was the candidate of Mabote's faction) and installed his own man, Merahe. *Round 2:* Mabote's group withheld their contributions to Merahe's wages, and in due course Merahe went on strike and precipitated a second crisis. This time the *lekgota* debate underlined the isolation of Mabote's faction, and the headman manoeuvred the District Commissioner into giving official backing to Merahe's wage-claim, and so, by implication, to his appointment. *Round 3:* This was not enough to secure Merahe's wages, and soon all attempts to control the borehole on a communal basis were abandoned. At last the District Councillor tried to solve the problem by transferring control of the borehole from the village authorities to the District Council.

The failure of the *lekgota* to solve this problem should be contrasted with their comparative success in making arrangements for the expansion of the school. In the latter case united action was possible because no section of the village had anything to gain at the expense of another, and because they were all dependent on the support of the District Commissioner, who was involved in the matter throughout. In the case of the *Borehole and the Pumpers*, on the contrary, jobs were at stake and the District authorities were not closely involved. The District Councillor's solution implied that they should be brought in.

v

The political process does not end with the making of a decision, or the failure to reach agreement on how to proceed on a matter. There is a feed-back to the social environment of the political system, and to the political system itself. Decisions may change the structure of authority, alienate certain groups or generate new support for the village government, or even give rise to new demands. Failures may create stresses—dissatisfaction with the village government or with the political system itself. The conflicts and stresses generated by the decision-making process may be briefly considered here.

I have returned several times to the constraints on the village political system created by the relationship with the District authorities. Before Botswana's independence, few demands from below were met, and support from above for the village government—in particular the headman—was unreliable. The inadequacy of support from above had repercussions on the conduct of village politics. In the normal course of events, a political decision had to be backed by a consensus if it was to be enforceable. It was occasionally possible for a group within the village to invoke the support of the District Commissioner or the police. The headman was best placed to do this, but the court-scribe and others might sometimes succeed in directing external force against their opponents. This was always risky, however, since the District authorities were remote and their intervention was spasmodic. Success in one issue might be purchased at the expense of the alienation of a group of villagers whose support would be necessary in another issue. In any case, the external authorities could not coerce villagers to cooperate with the headman, or even to attend *lekgota* meetings, and the headman often depended on their unforced commitment to a communal project. For their part, the villagers preferred in many instances to settle matters in their own way, and they resented undue interference from the external authorities. But since consensus was unlikely, for structural reasons, where internal policy matters were concerned, the *lekgota* was often hamstrung.

The problems involved in the relationship with the District authorities did not in themselves cause great stress within the village political system. The villagers did not hold the members of the village government responsible for unsatisfactory dealings with the District authorities, and the District authorities themselves were not inclined to introduce radical changes. The results of the Northern Kgalagadi experiment were not encouraging. Occasionally a District Commissioner might call for the appointment of 'younger, more go-ahead' headman and counsellors, but in general he contented himself with the knowledge that the village government did at least keep the peace and carry out the basic tasks of tax-collection and the administration of the law.

The need for consensus in the *lekgota*, and the inevitability of conflict on some issues, raised more serious and immediate difficulties. However, there have always been some mechanisms for damping down the expression of conflict, and these lessen the danger that conflict on one set of issues will prevent cooperation on another.

One such mechanism is the projection of the headman as the symbol of the unity of the village, and of the law. When conflicts become acute, some citizens will say that the headman is being challenged, which is a way of appealing to deep shared political values. The chief counsellor acts as the headman's spokesman, so protecting him from direct identification with any one point of view. The headman is expected to speak only when an agreed policy emerges from the debate. (The headman does sometimes take up a contentious position, but his followers often discourage him from doing so.) Direct attacks on the headman are rare. Even in the case of the *Headman and the Counsellor* the opposition was tactful and oblique.

The popularity of absenteeism as a political tactic is perhaps related to the fact that while it demonstrates opposition it avoids direct conflict. If one is absent from a *lekgota* meeting one cannot commit oneself to the support of a policy—but one is not forced to voice direct opposition.

Outsiders may be made to express unpopular or delicate decisions, or they may be used as scape-goats. The expulsion of the head-teacher from Kuli during a political crisis is a good example of the scapegoat mechanism at work. The neutral members of the village authority play roles comparable in many ways to those of the outsiders. They may force the *lekgota* to recognise and deal with delicate problems, and they sometimes bring into the open the workings of sectional interests, as Waatotsi exposed the tactics of Mabote's faction in the case of the *Borehole and the Pumpers*.

These and other mechanisms do not always succeed in containing conflict, but the village political system, as it was before 1966, showed great resilience. Because there was no obvious alternative, and because it served some useful functions, everybody was constrained to use the available political institutions and to accept the leadership of the headman, and he could fall back as a last resort on the backing of the District authorities.

These stresses were lessened with the advent of the District Councillors in 1966. The communication of demands to the District authorities improved, and the District Councillor was sometimes able to override factional conflicts in the *lekgota*. But these new developments brought with them new strains. In particular, there were sometimes problems of adjustment between the roles of headman and District Councillor. This was an acute issue in Kgalagadi District, but in Ghanzi District the District Councillor was able to secure his position without conflict, supported as he was by the citizen majority and the District Commissioner. The headman's judicial role and his ceremonial leadership were unchallenged.

Stress within the system may bring about changes, but radical changes in the village political system are more likely to be introduced from outside, as has been the case in the past. Botswana's political development, now as always, is shaped by developments in the east of the country, along the line of rail, in the new towns and the large Tswana reserves. The Botswana government is reported to be considering changes in the local government system in order to check the powers of the great Tswana chiefs. One cannot predict how such reforms will affect the west, with its different local political systems.

VI

I have been concerned mainly with one village, Kuli, but its political structure is similar to that of other Kgalagari and Tswana villages in Ghanzi District, and even to those of Northern Kgalagadi District, if one allows for the degree of centralisation and the police support for the sub-chief which are peculiar to that region. All these villages are characterised by a political balance between the headman, the citizens and Government; between the founding sub-clan and immigrant groups; and within the founding sub-clan between the headman and some of his close agnates. Factions exist in all villages, and are structured after the same fashion. Finally, each village polity is dominated by a small group of decision-makers, the authorities, who are recruited on similar principles. The political balance may be tipped this way or that by the proximity of a police post, special arrangements made by the District authorities, or peculiarities in the composition and organisation of immigrant communities in the village. These variations should not obscure the underlying similarity of the structure and process of Kgalagari politics throughout western Botswana. And perhaps this analysis will have wider applications. The structural factors I have isolated may have a fairly uniform significance throughout Africa—and beyond —even though they appear in a variety of cultural forms.

APPENDIX

CATTLE HOLDINGS AND VALUES

I

An official livestock census carried out in Kuli in the first quarter of 1967 by the cattle-guard, assisted by the court-scribe, revealed the following livestock holdings:

(a) Family-group heads

Name and group number	Cattle	Goats	Sheep
1. Ramošwane	179	160	34
2. Riphoni	102	173	35
3. Haudwelwe	80	8	—
4. Ramaseri	13	53	—
6. Molateši	37	24	—
7. Monantwe	51	153	—
8. Molede	9	23	—
9. Waatotsi	33	9	—
10. Moloise	59	13	—
11. Motojwane	—	110	—
12. Mabote	140	219	—
16. Mothibakgomo	45	112	—
17. Mokgethi	38	—	—
18. Masime	105	145	—
19. Modjathoši	64	28	—
20. Sebe	20	18	—
21. Tšekwe	28	64	—
22. Tatawane	19	80	—
23. Mahupunyane	27	21	—

It will be noticed that five of the twenty-four family-group heads in the village are not represented in this table. In the cases of two old men, Tsenene (13) and Mokeonyane (14), their sons are named, however, and may be taken to hold the family-group herds.

13. Morimomongwe	160	176	—
Lebiki	72	—	—
14. Salakae	47	68	—

With respect to the remaining three family-group heads, Mojakake (5) is a pauper; Kati (15) is a woman, and although women may have some livestock they are registered under the name of a man; and Bogope (24) is a recent immigrant, who may not yet have transferred his livestock to Kuli.

In addition to the family-group heads, twelve adult male villagers are registered as livestock holders:

(b) Other citizens

Name	Cattle	Goats	Sheep
Mogate	93	—	—
Ramuntšu	73	51	4
Sebetwane	35	37	—
Molapong	8	25	—
Teteme	16	46	—
Mokgosi	3	—	—
Gabokgalengwe	—	19	—
Phahane	8	—	—
Sebatamoze	42	33	—
Kedirikang	—	22	—
Ketloile	—	41	—
Thokamolomo	—	39	—

In most cases these are adult married who have earned money on migrant labour and bought livestock. Some have also been given stock by their fathers. A few are associates of family-groups, but the majority are members of their father's or father's brother's groups.

Finally, a few citizens of other villages keep some of their livestock in and around Kuli:

(c) Non-citizens

Name	Cattle	Goats	Sheep
Sehularo	—	33	—
Justus	—	1	—
Mongadi	102	53	—
Lekaukau	50	100	27
Moncho	2	—	—
Gaborone	9	—	—

This category includes two men from Hukuntsi and one from Ghanzi. The others come from less distant villages, and include the Kuli schoolmaster and assistants at stores in the District.

II

Taking all the figures together, the livestock holdings were as follows:

	Cattle	Goats	Sheep
Citizen holdings	1,606	1,960	73
Total holdings	1,769	2,147	100

A similar census carried out in September 1963 gives slightly lower figures, but does not include all the stockholders listed in the later census. However, it gives a breakdown of all categories of stockholdings which is of interest:

Cattle

Bulls		Cows	Heifers	Oxen	Tollies	Calves		Total cattle
Old	Young					Bulls	Heifers	
5	56	481	281	106	162	85	106	1,285

Other livestock

| Sheep | Goats | Horses | Mules | Donkeys | Poultry | Dogs |
| 66 | 1,339 | 85 | 2 | 88 | 97 | 34 |

III

The best prices for cattle are paid by the abattoir at Lobatsi, an enterprise in which Government has an interest. On the other hand, it is difficult and even dangerous to trek cattle right across the desert, and many people prefer to sell in small quantities to the local traders—but, of course, their prices tend to be low. A compromise is to wait for the occasional cattle-sales held in the District, or to sell heavily when a representative of one of the big buyers comes on a tour of the villages. Some idea of the value of cattle today may be gleaned from these figures of purchases made in Kuli in one day in October 1966 by a large buyer.

Mokgethi	1 ox	R40	Modjathoši	1 tolly	R18
	1 ox	R28		1 tolly	R16
Morimomongwe	2 oxen	R33 each	Ramuntšu	1 bull calf	R20
Tatawane	1 cow	R27		1 tolly	R25
Sekgome	1 cow	R23	Johannes	1 ox	R36
Salakae	1 cow	R25	Ramošwane	5 oxen	R30 each
Molateši	2 tollies	R21 each		1 ox	R27
Matlopelwe	1 tolly	R16		2 oxen	R24 each
Kelemile	1 tolly	R15			

BIBLIOGRAPHY

OFFICIAL PAPERS AND DOCUMENTS

Bechuanaland Protectorate. Annual reports.

——*Report of an Economic Survey Mission, Basutoland, Bechuanaland Protectorate and Swaziland*, London: HMSO, 1960.

——*Report on the Census of the Bechuanaland Protectorate*, 1964. Bechuanaland Government, 1965.

Bechuanaland Democratic Party. 'Objects and Principles' (n.d.). Mimeograph.

Newspapers, periodicals: *Therisanyo, Kutlwano*.

OTHER SOURCES

Barnes, Leonard. 1932. *The New Boer War*. London: Hogarth Press.

Breutz, P.-L. 1958. Ancient People in the Kalahari Desert. *Afrika und Ubersee*, vol. XLII, pp. 49–67.

Casalis, E. 1861. *The Basutos*. London: James Nisbet and Co.

Debenham, F. 1953. *Kalahari Sand*. London: G. Bell and Sons.

Dyson-Hudson, Neville. 1966. *Karimojong Politics*. Oxford: Clarendon Press.

Easton, David. 1959. 'Political Anthropology'. In *Biennial Review of Anthropology, 1959*. Ed. by Bernard J. Siegel. Stanford: Stanford University Press.

—— 1965. *A Systems Analysis of Political Life*. New York: Wiley.

Fallers, L. 1963. Political Sociology and the Anthropological Study of African Politics. *Archives Européennes de Sociologie*, vol. IV, no. 2, pp. 311–29.

Fortes, M. 1938. 'Culture Contact as a Dynamic Process'. In *Methods of Study of Culture Contact in Africa*, International African Institute Memorandum XV. Oxford: Oxford University Press.

—— 1940. 'The Political System of the Tallensi of the Northern Territories of the Gold Coast'. In *African Political Systems*. Ed. by M. Fortes and E. E. Evans-Pritchard. Oxford: Oxford University Press for the International African Institute.

—— 1962. 'Ritual and Office in Tribal Society'. In *Essays on the Ritual of Social Relations*. Ed. by Max Gluckman. Manchester: Manchester University Press.

Frankenberg, Ronald. 1966. *Communities in Britain*. Penguin Books.

Gluckman, Max. 1955. *The Judicial Process among the Barotse of Northern Rhodesia*. Manchester: Manchester University Press.

—— 1961. 'Ethnographic Data in British Social Anthropology'. *The Sociological Review*, vol. IX, no. 1, new series, pp. 5–17.

Gluckman, Max. 1963. *Order and Rebellion in Tribal Africa*. London: Cohen and West.

—— 1965. *The Ideas in Barotse Jurisprudence*. New Haven: Yale University Press.

Gluckman, Max, J. C. Mitchell and J. A. Barnes. 1949. The Village Headman in British Central Africa. *Africa*, vol. XIX, pp. 89–106. (Reprinted in Gluckman, 1963.)

Hailey. 1953. *Native Administration in the British Africa Territories*, Part Five. London: HMSO.

Hodgson, Margaret L. and Ballinger, W. G. (n.d. Probably 1931). *Britain in Southern Africa: (No. 2) Bechuanaland Protectorate*. Lovedale Press.

Hodson, A. W. 1912. *Trekking the Great Thirst*. London: T. Fisher Unwin.

Krige, E. J. and Krige, J. D. 1943. *The Realm of a Rain Queen*. Oxford.

Krige, Eileen Jensen. 1964. 'Property, Cross-Cousin Marriage, and the Family Cycle among the Lobedu'. In *The Family Estate in Africa*. Ed. by Robert F. Gray and P. H. Gulliver. London: Routledge and Kegan Paul.

Kuper, Adam. 1969a. The Kinship Factor in Ngologa Politics. *Cahiers d'Études Africaines*, no. 34, IX–2, pp. 290–305.

—— 1969b. The Work of Customary Courts: Some Facts and Speculations. *African Studies*, vol. 28, no. 1.

Leach, E. R. 1954. *Political Systems of Highland Burma*. London: G. Bell and Sons Ltd.

Leys, Colin. 1967. *Politicians and Politics*. Nairobi: East African Publishing House.

Livingstone, David. 1961. *Livingstone's Missionary Correspondence 1841–1856*. Ed. by I. Schapera. London: Chatto and Windus.

Mackenzie, J. 1871. *Ten Years North of the Orange River*. Edinburgh: Edmoston and Douglas.

Malinowski, B. 1938. Introductory Essay: 'The Anthropology of Changing African Cultures'. In *Methods of Study of Culture Contact in Africa*. International African Institute Memorandum XV. Oxford: Oxford University Press.

Political Systems and the Distribution of Power, ASA Monographs 2, London: Tavistock Publications. 1965.

Schapera, I. 1932. A Native Lion Hunt in the Kalahari Desert. *Man*, vol. XXXII, pp. 278–82.

—— 1935. The Social Structure of the Tswana Ward. *Bantu Studies*, vol. XI, pp. 203–24.

—— 1938. Ethnographic Texts in the Boloongwe Dialect of Sekgalagadi. *Bantu Studies*, vol. XII, pp. 157–87.

—— 1943. The Work of Tribal Courts in the Bechuanaland Protectorate. *African Studies*, vol. 2, pp. 27–40.

Schapera, I. 1950. 'Kinship and Marriage among the Tswana'. In *African Systems of Kinship and Marriage*. Ed. by A. R. Radcliffe-Brown and D. Forde. Oxford: Oxford University Press.

—— 1952. *The Ethnic Composition of Tswana Tribes*. London School of Economics Monographs on Social Anthropology, no. 11.

—— 1953. *The Tswana*. Ethnographic Survey of Africa. London: International African Institute.

—— 1955. *A Handbook of Tswana Law and Custom* (2nd edn). Oxford: Oxford University Press.

—— 1956. *Government and Politics in Tribal Societies*. London: Watts.

—— 1957. Marriage of Near Kin among the Tswana. *Africa*, vol. XXVII, pp. 139–59.

—— 1963a. 'Angatic Marriage in Tswana Royal Families'. In *Studies in Kinship and Marriage*. Ed. by I. Schapera. London: Royal Anthropological Institute.

—— 1963b. Kinship and Politics in Tswana History. *Journal of the Royal Anthropological Institute*, vol. 93, pp. 159–73.

Schapera, I. and van der Merwe, D. F. 1945. *Notes on the Tribal Groupings, History, and Customs of the Bakgalagadi*. Communications from the School of African Studies (new series, no. 13), University of Cape Town.

Sheddick, V. G. J. 1948. *The Morphology of Residential Associations as found among the Khwakhwa of Basutoland*. Communications from the School of African Studies (new series, no. 19), University of Cape Town.

Silberbauer, G. B. and Kuper, A. J. 1966. Kgalagari Masters and Bushman Serfs: Some Observations. *African Studies*, vol. 25, no. 4, pp. 171–9.

Sillery, A. 1952. *The Bechuanaland Protectorate*. Cape Town: Oxford University Press.

Southall, Aiden. 1965. 'A Critique of the Typology of States and Political Systems'. In *Political Systems and the Distribution of Power*, ASA Monographs no. 2. London: Tavistock.

Stow, G. W. 1905. *The Native Races of South Africa*. London: Sonnenschein.

Turner, V. W. 1957. *Schism and Continuity in an African Society: A Study of Ndembu Village Life*. Manchester: Manchester University Press.

Van der Merwe, D. F. and Schapera, I. 1943. *A Comparative Study of Kgalagadi, Kwena and other Sotho Dialects*. Communication of the School of African Studies (new series, no. 9), University of Cape Town.

Van Velsen, J. 1967. 'The Extended-case Method and Situational Analysis'. In *The Craft of Social Anthropology*. Ed. by A. L. Epstein. London: Tavistock.

Westphal, E. 1963. The Linguistic Prehistory of Southern Africa. *Africa*, vol. XXXIII, pp. 237–65.

INDEX

age-sets 43, 70, 107–8, 118
agriculture 19, 41, 145–6 *and passim*
authorities, village 17, 78–92, 103, 110, 118, 150, 167, 169, 171–2, 175–6, 179–80

Bechuanaland Protectorate, *see* Botswana
borehole 31, 41, 52, 53, 63, 71, 89, 103–4, 128, 131
  in politics 42, 89, 93–9, 115, 122–3
Botswana (former Bechuanaland Protectorate) 14, 19, 44–6, 132n, 143–4, 180
  history of 50–3
  independence of 16, 49, 56, 64, 92, 127, 168, 171–2, 178
Botswana Democratic Party (BDP)
  and district politics 57–9, 62, 85, 88, 168
  enters Kalahari 54–5
  names 54n
  policy of 47, 55–6
  and village politics 17, 62, 72, 93–100, 167–8, 171
bridewealth 34, 35, 36, 67, 82n, 91, 93, 136
Bushman (*see also* serfs) 7, 9, 10, 19, 28, 44–8, 51, 56, 71, 91, 93–9 *passim*, 103, 104–5, 106, 111, 157, 166, 171
  and law 134, 139–41, 141–3, 144–8 *passim*, 151–5, 162–3

Casalis 27, 88n
case-studies
  individual: Molateši 33–4; Waatotsi 34–6
  legal: the Rakile wife 135–7; a neighbourhood affair 138–9; a hungry bushman 139–41, 159, 164; the abducted wife 141–3, 151n; the border theft 143–4, 158, 175; the lady's cow 144–5; the widow's field 145–6; the sister's son 147–8; the jealous wife 148–9, 156–7; the brother's keeper 149–50, 161–2; the cheeky Bushman 147, 151–6, 158, 175

political: Kalkfontein succession dispute 66–9, 75, 78, 80; expansion of Kuli school 113–18, 176–7; borehole and pumper 119–24, 177, 179; unpaid fines 160–2, 176; headman and counsellor 124–7, 176, 179
cattle 5–6, 7, 12, 20, 24–5, 171
  discussed in *lekgota* 93–9
  posts 19, 34
  selling of 12, 40–1, 61, 62, 93–9, 104, 111–12, 114, 117, 122, 149, 183
  theft of 96–9, 103, 141, 145
  veterinary services 44, 95, 97, 99, 104
  and water 12, 103
  and wealth 87n, 181–3
Christianity and Christian Churches (*see also* London Missionary Society; prophets), 8, 42, 106, 136–7, 171
citizens 15, 17, 24, 71, 79, 103, 108, 167–80 *passim*
  and legal processes 134, 139, 141, 143, 144, 146, 150, 155–6, 159, 161, 163
  and policy-making 90–1, 110–31
  qualifications for 82n
clan 21, 22, 24, 25, 49
Council, District, *see* District Council
council, village 17, 19, 24, 25, 40, 43, 47, 55, 57, 62, 70, 71, 78, 80, 81, 82, 92, 167–80 *passim*
  attendance at 82–3, 85, 90–1
  behaviour in 110–11
  business of 93–109
  lekgota defined 141n
  meetings of, form 93
  policy-making in 110–31
council-place, village 22n, 79, 80, 150
  behaviour at 110–11
  described 110
counsellor, village 28, 61, 66, 69, 128–30, 137, 167, 172, 176, 179
  and decision-making 110, 115–17, 120
  and judicial process 132–65
  role described 78–81
court (*see also* council, village; moot) 40, 53, 74, 77, 108, 137, 138, 172
  committees of 139–43